TODAY'S
INSPIRED
Leader

TODAY'S INSPIRED LEADER

This book is a compilation of stories from people who have contributed a chapter and is designed to provide inspiration to our readers.

It is sold with the understanding that the publisher and the individual authors are not engaged in the rendering of psychological, legal, accounting or other professional advice. The content and views in each chapter are the sole expression and opinion of its author and not necessarily the views of Fig Factor Media, LLC.

For more information, contact:

Jaqueline Camacho-Ruiz
Fig Factor Media, LLC | www.figfactormedia.com
JJR Marketing, Inc. | www.jjrmarketing.com

Cover Design & Layout by Juan Pablo Ruiz
Printed in the United States of America

ISBN: 978-1-7324916-6-3

This book is dedicated to my mentors and all those who support others in achieving their dreams.

CONTENTS

ACKNOWLEDGEMENTS

I am filled with gratitude to the wonderful influencers, production team, and contributors that made this inaugural volume of *Today's Inspired Leader* possible. First of all, I want to acknowledge my present and past mentors who have helped me become the leader I am and, by association, helped me conceive of this project. I am grateful to the staff of JJR Marketing and especially to my life partner and creative director, Juan Pablo Ruiz, for the beautiful design and Karen Dix, for her editing and work with the authors. I am also grateful to each and every one of the contributing authors who believed in the vision of this book and strive in their daily work to elevate leadership in real and meaningful ways.

INTRODUCTION

On the heels of the international success of my anthology series, *Today's Inspired Latina*, I am excited to present *Today's Inspired Leader*. The idea of bringing together a collection of authors in an impactful anthology piece is not a new one, but it's an important way of giving voice to those who have stories and wisdom to share with the world.

Inside these pages are stories of revelation and wonder, tragedy and triumph, shared with vulnerability and determination. This is a book born out of love, raised with care and delivered to the world with pride and purpose. My hope is that everyone will find the words of a mentor within these pages and the encouragement and fortitude to press on and become the best leader they can possibly be. In that way, *Today's Inspired Leader* will become a gift to us all!

PREFACE

By Greg Cox
Founder and CEO of The Impact Foundry, Inc.

My first encounter with Jackie Camacho-Ruiz was through an enthusiastic voicemail. I didn't connect with her until some time later, but I remember that message. You remember your first encounter with Jackie. I first connected with her when she was helping with marketing and branding for a non-profit I was involved in, The Sheilah A. Doyle Foundation. Soon she was developing marketing campaigns for the major training organization I led. I had the privilege of getting to know Jackie and working with her talented and dynamic team.

When I decided to open my own consulting firm, one of my first calls was to Jackie. Her passion to see entrepreneurs succeed helped launch my company. She helped me get clear on my business concept, designed my website, and developed the branding that still gets me excited every time I see it. She captured the images I wanted to convey and helped me take my story to the marketplace. For me, Jackie has been a business partner, a collaborator, and an encourager.

Jackie has a calling to help people pursue their dreams and passions. She finds joy in inspiring people to go to a place they would not go on their own. She loves to bring the "amazing" not just to companies and organizations, but into people's lives. Whether she is helping an established corporation breathe new life into their message, helping a new entrepreneur launch their dream, flying a plane, or inspiring young Latinas, Jackie never attacks projects half-heartedly. That same enthusiasm and vision for seeing leaders take their game to the next level is what has fueled this book.

Leaders can benefit greatly from an honest, insightful coach. Without the insight from others, we can easily lose our focus and pursue things that only distract us from our goals. We can easily get off track and end up busy, but ineffective. We need the wise counsel of a few trusted advisors who can point out our blind spots, help us see what is tripping us up, and clarify our vision. We can't listen to just any advice. We must choose our coaches carefully. We need someone who has experience, wisdom, insight, and candor. This book will introduce you to a team of leadership veterans who can share their best practices and stories from the field with you. Listen to them. Learn from them.

I am a firm believer that leaders need to be readers. Only through continuing to learn and challenge ourselves can we be effective, dynamic leaders. We must be life-long, passionate learners if we want to influence others and take them to a place they would not go on their own. That is why I am excited about this collection of leadership insights. Each contributor has a unique voice and a tremendous message to communicate. We can learn so much through the experiences and insights of others, especially those who have sought to grow their own leadership skills and desire to see others do the same.

The unique format of this book lets you hear the advice

and wisdom of many people. Jackie has compiled these insights from men and women who have impacted her. In keeping with her passion to inspire others, she has chosen these leaders to share their wisdom, advice, insights, and experiences. Jackie has a unique ability to connect people and make "magic" happen. This book connects you to a whole group of people who can inspire and encourage you in whatever vision you are pursuing.

Read this book. Underline it. Mark it up. Keep it on your desk. Give copies away. But most importantly, live it. Our world needs constructive, inspiring, and positive leadership. In the words of Marshall Goldsmith, "What got you here won't get you there." So, how do you get "there?" This book is your roadmap.

Greg Cox
Founder and CEO of The Impact Foundry, Inc.
www.theimpactfoundry.com
info@theimpactfoundry.com

Gretchen,

You are amazing and you matter a whole lot.

I love you. Yesterday, today and always.

Cheers,

05/26/19

IT MATTERS MORE THAN YOU THINK

Gabriela Rodil

"Our impact goes much further than
we can anticipate."

The year was 2014. I remember it was a Tuesday. I came into the office expecting another normal work day. Keep in mind what constitutes "normal" for me may not be seen that way by others. At that point, I had been the CFO for a 550+ employee multinational manufacturer for more than three years. I was responsible for accounting, finance, treasury, legal, IT, among other departments. My days were dynamic to say the least and filled with challenges and sometimes, curve balls. Like the day I had to respond to an unemployment claim filed by an employee who had been dismissed with cause for punching another employee. That was especially surprising given that we had the event on tape. Despite all the unpredictability, I loved the job.

THE VISIT

I had no reason to think that Tuesday would be any different, so I went about my day. Around lunch time, one of the plant supervisors came into my office and asked to speak to me. I asked Amy to come in, close the door and take a seat. Amy told me she was there to tender her resignation. I was surprised by it for two reasons: (1) Why would she be resigning after only seven months on the job when all I had heard about her performance and impact was positive? (2) Why was she coming to me when she could have gone to her manager, the head of the department, or human resources?

Like many times before in my life, I decided to roll with it. With my "CFO hat" placed firmly on my head, I asked a few clarifying questions to understand if there were deeper issues at play. I wanted to find out if there had been an event triggering her decision to resign. I wanted to know if this was an isolated event or a symptom of a larger problem in the company. I was also looking for information that would allow me to assess the company's exposure and potential liability related to personnel changes.

There was nothing in what Amy was telling me that pointed to a systematic issue or incident. She made it clear it had nothing to do with the company and that she wanted to do something different with her life. I told her I could not make her stay and that I would respect her final decision. I was ready to accept her resignation and have HR take care of the paperwork.

But something told me that wasn't enough. Amy had

come to me, someone who had not been involved in her hiring, management, or was even part of the hierarchy structure she reported into. I don't believe in coincidences; I take whatever comes my way as an opportunity/challenge. I assume everything that happens is a chance to succeed or to learn a lesson. All experiences have a purpose and ultimately contribute to making us better.

With that in mind, I decided to take off my CFO hat and just talk to her so we could connect as human beings. I wanted her to understand how she was seen and how important her contribution was to the company. I shared with her what I had heard from other people about her: she was doing a great job, the department was running smoothly, her employees were happy with her leadership, etc. I shared with her about the many times I had been overwhelmed or doubted myself in my own career, and I would be disappointed to see such a talented person walk away. It would be a great loss for the company too, and I told her I believed that every problem has a solution and there is always a way to make things better. I told her that I believe we are all works in progress and should always be observing, learning, and finding different ways to look at challenges.

I mentioned other alternatives that were potentially available for her. Since Amy was an employee in good standing, the company could make reasonable accommodations. I asked Amy to consider taking a leave of absence to deal with any personal matters or to explore job opportunities in other departments inside the company. I reiterated that her options were not "all or nothing" and invited her to rethink the decision and be open to other solutions besides quitting.

Amy took it all in and told me she would be willing to stay, and we could figure things out together. We talked for almost an hour. We agreed to an outline of a plan to make sure she was getting the support she needed. I engaged human resources and made sure I continued to follow up and monitor the situation. As a leader it is still your responsibility to solve an issue even if you didn't cause it.

The conversation with Amy got me thinking about the many moments in my career when I felt overwhelmed, started doubting myself, or felt I was not good enough. That little voice inside one's head that says they will not choose you, they will find a better candidate when applying for a job or I don't look good enough when you are getting ready in the morning, or if people knew the real me, they wouldn't like me or have confidence in my abilities. I remembered the feeling when I started as CFO in that company. It was the highest position I had ever held at the time. I was afraid I might not measure up and meet the expectations. For the first time in my career, I felt I was operating without a safety net; the buck stopped with me. In contrast to being one of the many consulting managers at a large firm, I was the "last word" in finance, accounting, etc.

The little voice in my head got louder. There is so much riding on this! What was I thinking? CFO, yeah right! What if you mess this up? The fear of failing and imagining that people would "know" I failed can be paralyzing. I knew that if I remained in in my head dialoguing exclusively with myself, I would get nowhere.

I did what I frequently advise others to do – talk to other people. I reached out to my network, former managers, formal and informal mentors, and friends. I shared my fears, dilemmas, questions, and doubts. And I allowed them to remind me of my own capabilities and qualities. One of my mentors said, "Trust me when I say they are lucky to have you and they don't even know." Coming from him, this sentiment meant the world to me. I developed a relationship with the head of departments at my job. I worked to create an environment of collaboration and learning. I asked many questions, even if I was afraid it was a "stupid" question. Prefacing questions with "this may be a simple question, but…" or "remind me again about"… can take the pressure off asking. How I ask a question puts others and myself at ease. I reminded myself of my own achievements and took deep breaths when I needed to get centered and do my best work. Over time, the voices subsided, my confidence grew, and I was able to put forth great work.

Amy was able to do the same after our meeting. She went back to work and continued to do great. She finished reorganizing and streamlining a crucial department in the production process. That department had been a bottleneck in the past and was the source of high levels of waste and rework. The results were great: optimized inventory, faster lead time, happier customers, and lower costs.

I thought that was the end of my story with Amy until

seven or eight months after that Tuesday, Amy came into my office again. She asked for a few minutes of my time and again, she came in, closed the door and sat down. She told me how thankful she was for our conversation months earlier and she thanked me for helping her and for being supportive and understanding that day. She expressed she wasn't sure what she would have done had I not pushed her to rethink her choice and get re-engaged with her work. When we first met, she was feeling desperate, struggling with many personal problems, and considering some extreme measures.

I was shocked by her revelations. I had no idea what was going on with her during that first meeting. I told her she was welcome and thanked her for being open and flexible, for allowing herself to change her mind. I was grateful for the opportunity to be there for her when she needed it, even though I didn't know the details.

It's easy to see how our first conversation had been impactful for her and ultimately, life- changing. However, the second time we sat down to talk, it was life changing for me. I was able to instantly and viscerally understand the impact we have on others. Even if we don't know how or when the things we do and say, both big and small, may impact others in unexpected ways. Our impact goes much further than we can anticipate, especially when we are in charge.

THE BUTTERFLY EFFECT

I believe we never truly know the full extent of our effect

on others. It is great when we receive feedback about how something we did or said impacted someone else. I am grateful for the times it has happened to me and I make sure I let people know how they influenced me and how thankful I am for their contribution in my life.

It doesn't stop there. The people we impact go on to create impact in their own lives and the lives of others. We send out ongoing waves of impact into the world. Even if we don't know where it ends up, we can be sure we have impacted others in some way. It is the butterfly effect! That's the idea that small things can have non-linear impacts on a complex system. The concept is imagined with a butterfly flapping its wings in Chicago and causing a tornado in Tokyo, for example.

I consider myself very lucky. I have only been able to do what I do and be where I am because of the many people that were or who are part of my life. It begins with the nurturing family I was lucky enough to be born into. My parents valued education, and I was fortunate to be able to dedicate time to mine. Curiosity was revered. We kept a dictionary and an atlas next to the dining room table to use regularly as reference in conversations.

Today there are a variety of learning sources. I continue to learn and expand through them: books, podcasts, TED talks, documentaries, etc. The key is to be selective given the sheer volume of information available.

I also had great teachers and professors who were patient and took the time to answer my many questions outside the classroom. I wanted to learn everything I could, and I wanted to explore options and different ways of looking at things. A habit that continues today.

When I started to work, I paid attention to the people around me. I observed their behavior, how they talked to others, and how they presented themselves. I quickly learned that there is no "one size fits all" approach when it comes to interactions. If you take the time to understand people's style, preferences and stay cognizant of their state of mind, you will develop relationships, be more effective and have a much better time at work.

I sought managers who were willing to formally or informally mentor me. I worked to understood what their needs were and how I could make their lives easier. Not only did I learn a lot just by doing this, but the people I helped were more open to training, coaching, and mentoring me. I paid close attention and took detailed notes. I never wasted people's time so they would be willing to continue to help me.

I was lucky to have an amazing manager at my first internship. The manager was Ricardo Pelegrin, a veteran consultant and a great teacher. I was in my third year of business school. When I look back, I can see how "green" I was, but I made up for it with how excited and eager I was to learn. He was the first person in my career to see my potential and mentor me. He taught me about the world of consulting, he encouraged me and made me part of his team, he showed me how to make financial models in Excel using advanced formulas and macros, and he coached me on how to interact with colleagues and clients in a more effective way. He didn't allow me to get away with anything. It was not pleasant to have someone point out your weak spots, but he did it constructively made me accept it and improve. The butterfly effect of his leadership continues to make me who I am today.

I also learned to volunteer to be part of many projects or tasks. My philosophy is to say "yes," then work it out. Of course, I felt overwhelmed at times and regretted some of the work I said "yes" to completing. But when I look back, even when things didn't go according to plan or were a complete disaster, I still learned something from it. Rahul Sharma said it best: "Forget the mistake and remember the lesson. For the mistake can be ignored, but not the lesson."

RELATIONSHIPS COUNT

It is crucial to continuously develop relationships and connect with people like family, friends, neighbors, clients, vendors, colleagues, etc. I love having people to count on, to bounce ideas around, process issues with, be encouraged by, learn from, etc. I strive to play that same role for others. The lesson I learned from my interaction with Amy and continue to apply today is a simple one. Stop and take the time to connect with others, ask a few questions, change your approach and to go deeper. Seconds or minutes can have a great impact. Take a step back, listen to the little voice in your head, think outside the box, and think beyond your function and procedures. Look inside yourself and connect with the other person. Allow yourself to be understanding, compassionate, and kind. Ask yourself if you are being the person you want to be. If you feel you didn't "get it right" the first time, go for a do over. Sometimes it only takes apologizing or clarifying.

I understand that we live in a fast-paced world and we frequently operate under real, or perceived, time constraints. This is why it is even more important to slow down, take a step back, and make sure you are incorporating some of your humanity into what you do. In the long run, it saves you time.

MENTORSHIP MOMENT

Leaders are always in a unique position to impact their team members' lives in many significant ways, just as others have impacted theirs. Living with self-awareness, intentionality, gratitude and humility can help you become the best leader you can be. Consider these questions to assess how you are impacting or can make a positive difference in other people's lives.

1. In what situations in my life could I step outside of myself and allow my human side to shine through?
2. Who do I want to be? How do I want to impact other people's lives?
3. How do I want to be remembered?
4. Is there any situation I would like to rectify? What first step can you take towards doing that?
5. Who would I like to thank for contributing to my life?

BIOGRAPHY

Gabby Rodil is an award-winning entrepreneur, international speaker, author, and gifted CFO with deep expertise in the critical areas of financial strategy, systems management, and Merger & Acquisitions. She is originally from Brazil, speaks six languages, and has lived and worked in more than 20 countries.

She is founder and CEO of Gabriela Rodil & Co., which provides strategic consulting to small and mid-size business. The firm helps clients by developing and implementing value creation plans involving finance, IT and operations; preparing companies to go to market; or leading the selection, implementation, or revamping of their ERP systems. Gabby is dedicated to increasing the value of organizations in constantly dynamic and changing environments.

As a speaker, Gabby's high energy style and stories from the front lines impact audiences and change lives. She helps leaders reach their organization's potential by connecting their vision, people, and operations in revealing and unconventional ways.

Gabby is a board member and treasurer of The Fig Factor Foundation. She is a co-author of the book *Today's Inspired Latina* and has been featured on many media outlets such as WGN Adelante Chicago with Lourdes Duarte, INC, Halfstack, and Illinois CPA magazines.

Gabriela Rodil

gabby@gabrielarodil.com

(302) 206-4542

UNLIMITED THINKER

Mary K. Mathis

"People call you delusional until you start getting paid for it."

I'm a dual national, American and Australian, serial entrepreneur, global traveler, creative writer, challenge seeker, sailor, and dog lover. I am a strong proponent for advancing women in society and in the workplace. I have extreme optimism and grit, two qualities imperative for success. The one thing I know for sure is that only love is real.

I've come to believe that my "why," or purpose for being, is to demonstrate the power of unlimited thinking.

I also believe that women's stories can change the world.

PIONEERING SPIRIT

Leaders are people that know how to forge into the unknown, bringing people with them, following their mission with confidence, enthusiasm, and courage. I certainly have a track record for forging into the unknown, and I come by this pioneering spirit honestly.

I grew up in Florida, the middle child born to a New England Democrat mother, and a Southern Republican father. Naturally, we fought the Civil War in our home. My great grandparents drove down from Chicago in a Model T Ford at the turn of the century and settled in what was then Lemon City in Miami, living in a boarding house and dining in communal tents. My grandmother, "Nana Kathleen," survived the 1926 hurricane at the age of 12 by holding onto a palm tree. My great grandmother, Big Nana, and her sister, Aunt Maude, were audacious linotype setters for the Miami newspaper who smoked, drove cars, and embroidered their teddies.

My older brother contracted spinal meningitis at 18 months, when treatment had not yet evolved, resulting in some brain damage, coordination difficulties and frequent grand mal epileptic seizures. My younger sister was a competitive, Olympic-bound gymnast with asthma. Babysitters were reluctant to take on our family challenges and often, I was awarded the task, which eventually included rescuing my older brother from bullies at school, an attempted lynching, and other acts of human ignorance and cruelty.

I developed advanced communication and negotiating skills early; not to mention, a wry sense of humor.

Having grown up (mostly) in Miami, I chose to attend Hollins, an isolated, private, all-women's university outside of

Roanoke, Virginia. There I studied English and political science with the aim of becoming a lawyer, but I also read voraciously and studied creative writing with a passion. This ultimately clashed with my father's aspirations for me, however it expanded my horizons in a wildly different direction from my peers.

I have been blessed with amazing women role models, mentors, and guides. From an early age these included my mother, Alice Lorraine, whose unique combination of courage, silly humor, patience, and perseverance was immeasurable, and her older sister, my Aunt Anita, a highly intuitive, spiritual, and wellness-enlightened beauty, who taught me to "aim high" and "keep trading up."

Marina Polvay, my mentor, took me under her wing right out of college, where I started out as a ghostwriter. Marina and her stable of senior food and travel writers who were off on another trip assignment, would throw me their notes and I formulated them into the designated voice, length, and format for various magazines. Marina was a boss and adopted "mother" figure, Russian-born royalty that spoke nine languages. Marina wrote for food and travel magazines, published over a dozen cookbooks, hosted television and radio shows, and was a leading hospitality and public relations consultant, outrageous storyteller, gambler, and raconteur.

She took me to New York City every month to meet with editors and producers to learn the art of marketing and communications, and in Miami she had me staging parties for Richard Burton, the Jewish Mafia, and the Saudi Arabian Royal family. Before I was 24, Marina sent me around the world twice as a writer and hired me again when I returned from Australia and the Pacific Rim, after an absence of 14 years.

I was 21 when she taught me an important lesson: anything is possible, but some things cost more than others.

I was having a pretty good life when, through an event that Marina staged, I met a blue-eyed, Italian-Australian with the last name of Martini -- and my global adventure took a twist.

We married in 1984, thinking we were moving to Jordan, where he had been offered a position as palace manager for King Hussein and Queen Noor in the number two palace in Aqaba. My only request was to be able to bring my electric typewriter, a home computer (a new innovation at the time), and my cat, as I was going to write the inside story of the Royal Family. (The cat was denied.)

The PLO was staging unrest in the region, and my fresh husband simultaneously received an offer to join a fledgling hotel group back in his native Perth, Western Australia – the most isolated city in the world. I was young enough to practice "whither thou goest," and off I went. Marina didn't speak to me for two years.

THE MARTINI GROUP

There I was, Mary Martini, in a place where I couldn't understand what the people were saying, and I had to learn to drive on the other side of the road and live with my rather large mother-in-law who did not speak English.

I did the only thing I knew how to do: I set up a marketing and public relations firm in a country where I knew no one.

My first client was American Express. They wanted me (through a publisher) to write a national restaurant guide. The second client was an energetic, dark-skinned, Malaysian-Indian who was launching newspapers at the time of the great newspaper wars in Australia when Fairfax, Holmes a Court, and Bond were all at each other's throats. There were virtually no dark-skinned people in Perth then, and this man was not only brilliant, but also wealthy and outrageous. We had some building bomb scares, hired a strange mix of ex-athletes and heroin addicts (they make great sales people for short periods of time), made some noise, and in doing so, I built a company.

Then, Alan Bond, an Australian, with his Boxing Kangaroo icon, won the America's Cup yacht race for the first time in 132 years. The Cup was leaving New York for Perth and Fremantle, just south, where the next International 12-Metre yacht race was to be held.

Never display competency, for you will be given a job. Seems like I might have been the only wildly enthusiastic, optimistic-to-the-point-of-being-almost-delusional event planner, marketer and public relations professional in 1984 in the most isolated city in the world. The Royal Perth Yacht Club was expecting over 3,000 guests including royalty, heads of state, CEOs of major corporations, celebrities, sailors, and yes, the Aga Khan.

By then, it was the Martini Group (my friends wanted

to be known as Debbie Daiquiri and Margot Margarita) and we took the project on with seven employees, IBM electric typewriters, 500 couriers, and 1,000 contractors. There was no facility large enough at the time to host the event and I looked to leveling land and converting abandoned factories.

The America's Cup Cocktail party in 1986 and the America's Cup Ball in 1987 put Australia on the map, but my marriage was in tatters. I got divorced and took on more clients.

Divorce is hard. I know, I've done it twice. One must try to make good informed life choices, while remembering that there really are no mistakes and each chapter leads to another. Being divorced in a country of adoption means you have to make a stand to justify why you are in the position you are in – in this case, alone and a foreigner. I stood up and owned my decisions - stubbornly and with conviction. I had to choose to stay and build or run home and find what was familiar. As a post note on this discussion of life partners and life choices, I am currently married to my greatest partner and mentor, a lawyer, a leader, and a great man who supports me in my every endeavor. I consider all else before him, my teachers, lessons and place holders, as guides who brought me to the joy we have today.

ICARUS MOMENT

One of the dumbest things I've ever done was to buy a business I knew nothing about, simply because I liked the services. In the early 90's, my marketing business was booming. To balance the frenetic work pace, I attended an upmarket salon for facials and massages in what later became the Hyatt hotel. The owner was pregnant and wanted to sell. I was a good, regular client but was clueless about the beauty industry. After negotiations and inventory taking, where I truly demonstrated my ignorance, I took possession and named the place "Madame Lillian." I thought it sounded European, but it only triggered a visit by the local, leading brothel owner to see if I was the competition.

A month after I took over, the former owner's manager left with all the clients. For me, the beauty business was far from beautiful -- the whole venture was a struggle that lasted too long and sapped my resources at every level. The moral of the story is that you should know or learn a lot about a business before you buy it, make sure your ego is parked at the door, and make a prudent investment with thorough legal and accounting assistance and deep-dive due diligence. Surround yourself with top-notch advisors who understand you better than you understand yourself.

THE MINING BUSINESS

I had (for the region at that time) considerable experience in the business world and hospitality industry, between the work I had done with Marina and my ex-husband's hotel business. Furthermore, I had recently learned a harsh lesson about research and due diligence. People trusted me with incredibly interesting and strange projects. A wealthy Australian attorney friend paid me to drive eight hours into the red desert of the Nullarbor Plain with an American Indian, a Russian reeking of vodka, and an entrepreneur who had recently been released from a mental institution. At the request of the entrepreneur, my friend was considering investing in a tailings operation in Kalgoorlie, the gold mining epicenter of Western Australia. Tailings are the materials left over after the process of separating the valuable fraction from the undesirable part of an ore. It was a rare and fascinating experience, but I advised firmly against the investment.

The brother of a friend of mine was building a hotel in Bali. The architect for the project had never been to Bali and there had been no market research or feasibility study conducted. I pointed out the naiveté of this business approach rather directly and, sure enough, was given a job and a piece of the action.

In Bali, I put together a strategic team to implement a concept for a resort based on what the Aga Kahn had done with the Costa Smerelda in Sardinia. I had been sent to Sardinia by an Arkansas-based merchant banker to attend the World 12-Metre yacht races to maintain the connections he had made in Perth and Fremantle. My team and I travelled several times to Bali and proceeded to commence work without first securing a significant deposit from the developer client. The client was waiting on the transfer of funds from an outside investor and had taken loans against his home, as had all of the development team, to fund the project so far.

At the time, Bali was under the rule of a strong, military-backed government. It was said that the dominant ruling family was in the "mining business" – more specifically, "this is mine, this is mine, and this is mine." They decided the hotel project was going to be theirs, and there was little recourse for my team or the Australian developers who lost their homes. I lost 50,000 dollars, and fortunately, was able to secure a loan from a Commonwealth Development bank. It was another hard lesson learned about speculation, trust, enthusiasm for a project, and practical evaluation of "risk versus reward."

The Martini Group eventually represented more than 200 oil and gas and mining companies and created a statewide event called "Minerals and Energy Week" to highlight and showcase the intrinsic role of mining and exploration in job creation and the economy.

We also became very involved in crisis management, property development, environmental relations, federal airport development, the South Sea pearling industry, Aboriginal Affairs, federal elections, and special events like the Golden Oldies Rugby Festival, where we staged a three-course sit down dinner for 7,000 guests.

We did this with a very tight and dedicated team with an elastic ability to think outside of the box, figure out how to overcome obstacles, and operate like cheerful problem solvers.

Then the recession hit, and I relocated to Malaysia.

RESTARTS AND REINVENTIONS

The Universe has a master plan. It may not be the one you have in mind. There is an art to reinvention. First, you must take a really good look at yourself and your situation. Find people you can trust to guide you, and then become a profound listener. You can build a better life by letting go of your old one. For every decision you make in your life, the seeds of self-destruction are planted within. Life is full of seasons, and all of life's energy is intertwined.

"*Selamat Datang*" means welcome in Bahasa Malay. My former client in the newspaper business had moved to Malaysia with his Australian wife. They welcomed me like family and created a world of comfort and opportunity in Kuala Lumpur. In Bali, I had learned about Hindu and Buddhist traditions. In "KL," I was to learn the Muslim, Chinese, and Bumiputra ways.

I stayed in Kuala Lumpur on and off for years, working an array of dazzling projects and seeing a side of deal making in the heart of the Tiger economy of Singapore and Southeast Asia. I also kept a footprint in Australia and had begun to aggregate some property.

During these years, my father passed away and I lost two fiancés, one to lung cancer and another to a massive heart attack. I had accomplished much in my 14 years away from the States, and had thought many times of returning to live, although I regularly did the 26-hour commute flight.

I had big plans to form a global alliance connecting Perth with Southeast Asia and Miami with Latin America. In 1997, on a trip to the States, I sealed a deal to set up shop back in Miami and secured a giant job. The very night I returned to Oz from the trip, my world changed irrevocably. I had previously experienced times of tremendous loss and trauma and, in coping, had developed a blend of spiritual balance and practicality. That night, a home invasion that turned dark left me broken and fearful. Once again, I was on a path of change and reinvention.

I returned to Miami in 1998 with my golden retriever named "The Amazing Grace" and settled on an island called Brickell Key. Islands are a recurring theme in my destiny. I set a goal of living without fear. I adopted a new routine of meditation, exercise, time in nature, and breathing. Still, culturally I was an alien who didn't fit in. My old friends were all in the suburbs, raising their kids, while I had been the Indiana Jones of the Pacific Rim.

You are what you attract. It's good for you to stretch your brain beyond your comfort zone. I bought a home in South Florida, another golden retriever named "One of These Days Alice," married for nine years, divorced, and at last met a soulmate who shares my life and the business in New York and Florida.

The Japanese art of kintsugi teaches that broken objects are not something to hide but display with pride. I strive to frame challenges in a positive way, always looking for the silver lining. This philosophical approach to my new life back in the States was useful in staying on track to find my feet, reconnect with family, build friendships as well as create a vision for new business and growth opportunities.

My husband and I travel, enjoy life, invest in some start-ups and explore technology. We settled into our home on the beach in Florida and spent three years rebuilding an 85-year-old, two-story landmark – a symbol of reconstruction and an amalgamation of tastes, treasures, and stories. It's a symbol of new stability, a foundation ready for friends and extended family. We bought a puppy, and you guessed it, it's an English Cream golden retriever we named "Asia Paloma." We also keep an apartment in Manhattan.

It would appear I have come full circle at this juncture. I spend a lot of time in personal development and professional growth. Forming key alliances and partnerships is crucial, and I have been laser-focused on selecting those people and organizations that are aligned with my vision. I am an ardent proponent for the advancement of women in our workplace and our society. I intend to use my life's experiences and insights to bring vision and leadership into ventures that promote and enhance women, to share their stories, and to cultivate gender equality and diversity in the workplace.

People call you delusional until you start getting paid for it. Then, they call you brilliant. I learned to relax and got to better know the blend of qualities that are unique to me. Now I take the time to carefully assess where they can be deployed, properly, with efficiency and enthusiasm. Life is fun! And filled with second chances. Who knew?

After a few business ventures and some personal adaptations, I launched a new business celebrating cultural diversity and helping women navigate more than one culture. It is called *Latinarrific*!

It is a journey I understand.

MENTORSHIP MOMENT

1. Develop healthy rituals:
    - Rise at the same time each morning
    - You can change your entire day with a breath. Learn the art of breathing.
    - Practice unbridled optimism.
    - Eat more veggies.
    - Drink 1-2 liters of water daily.
    - Get as much sleep as you can.
    - Stretch your body. Stretch your mind.
    - Walk in nature, absorb the energy.
    - Unplug regularly.
    - Find what gives you joy and follow it – joy is not the same as instant gratification.
    - Learn the art of patience and self-control.
    - Develop daily affirmations and attach an emotion to each one.
    - Know when to be nice.

2. If you focus on hitting the rock – you will hit the rock.
3. Find good advisors. Surround yourself with people who are smarter than you are.
    - The best lessons in life come from experience: someone else's!
    - Your good advisors will rain on your parade. Listen profoundly.

- Find some positive thinkers and reinforcements to offer you encouragement along the way.
- The right partner can multiply your potential.

4. Maintain a sense of humor. In essence, find what makes you laugh in a tough situation.
5. If you think you are being underestimated, use it to your advantage.
6. Embrace diversity.
7. Read: *The Seat of the Soul*, Gary Zukov; *Start With Why*, Simon Sinek; *The Power of Full Engagement*, Jim Loehr and Tony Schwartz; *Think Bigger*, Michael Sonnenfeldt
8. Remember, if were easy, everyone would be doing it.

BIOGRAPHY

Mary K. Mathis, founder and CEO of Latinarrific, is a serial entrepreneur and dual national (American and Australian) who truly understands biculturalism.

Mary has more than 25 years of experience and demonstrated expertise in international management, marketing, operations, sales, emerging technologies and integrated strategic communications. She was previously CEO of an international management, marketing, and public relations firm located in the U.S., Australia, Malaysia, and Indonesia. The firm also acted as a venture capital and investment company and assisted with international trade facilitation and cultural and technological exchange.

In 2004, she acquired a streaming media technology company and established CBC.TV, an internet television venture, and the parent company of Mensaje Media. She recognized early the confluence of a growing Hispanic community and underserved market of Latina programming in the U.S., and the importance of marketing to this minority group with more than 1.5 trillion dollars' worth of buying power.

Mary has a special passion for empowering women. Her most recent venture is Latinarrific, an inspirational, transformational platform to help the American Latina be her best bicultural self. It is the only digital presence dedicated to Latina storytelling and officially launched on September 15, 2016 as part of Hispanic Heritage Month.

Mary K. Mathis
mmathis@latinarrific.com
(954) 224-2296
LinkedIn: /marymathislatinarrific

LIFE'S LADDER

——

Jennifer Wilken

"When you see a person climbing the steps of life's ladder, influence them to keep climbing."

There are endless analogies we could use to describe the twists and turns and ups and downs of life. Many people refer to this as their personal journey. I like to think of it all as a ladder-life's ladder.

Throughout my career, I have climbed up and down the steps of the ladder of life, gathering experience and learning lessons. I am thankful for the relationships I have gained along the way and the profound influence they have had on me. I want to thank the influencers who helped me along life's ladder: my parents, business mentors, personal mentors, friends, peers, and those I have mentored.

With decades of experience under my belt, what excites me now is the opportunity to become an influencer of others. I want to know what I can do to expedite someone's climb up the ladder.

Over the years, I have mentored and coached many of my

peers. However, only recently, my former mentees have been sharing something I said or did that helped them along their career path. Sometimes, I would recall the moment they were sharing with me, but more often, I did not remember it. I found myself embarrassed, and yet fascinated with how something insignificant to me could leave such an impact on another. This made me realize that by being more intentional with mentoring and coaching, I could have an even greater impact and inspire others to be influencers too.

LEAN TIMES AND HARD WORK

I come from a family with a military background. My mom served in the Army and my dad served in the Navy. My brother served in the Army for six years, and his three children are all currently serving in the Army. I am the first college graduate in my family.

I grew up with two working parents. My dad was a sales engineer and is one of the smartest guys I know. He worked a typical nine to five job and he also served as a board member of a nonprofit organization in our community. My mom was in and out of the hospital as I was growing up. She had a number of health problems which led to multiple surgeries and hospital stays. Despite her circumstances, she was always willing to help others and often invited family and friends to move into our home when they were in need.

My parents were homeowners, but money was very tight when I was growing up, especially if my mom was unable to work.

Bill collectors called and even came to our house. I recall going to the orthodontist and overhearing the staff discuss how we owed them money. I wore braces for three years, much longer than necessary, simply because we did not have the means to pay the bills. Living paycheck to paycheck was our way of life. Clearly, my parents were not in a position to save money for college. My brother—two-years older than me—had every intention of pursuing military service and using the GI bill to pay for college.

My parents and I applied for and received loans for my college tuition and fees. In order to cover additional expenses, I worked as a nanny for five kids, cleaned houses, served pizza, and worked on campus. During my college years, I implemented a "work hard, play hard" type of schedule which I didn't recognize as unusual until I was much older. I graduated from Southern Illinois University in May of 1992 with a bachelor of arts in political science. My intention was to work a few years to pay down the student loans and credit cards while I figured out a path to law school.

My first real job was as an assistant in an insurance office. I became an associate agent where I was responsible for the client contact, paperwork, underwriting, and administrative work for several insurance agents. My dad pointed out that I had the same level of education and I was close in age to the agents I assisted. He encouraged me to move up the ladder and work for myself. He said if they could do it, I could too.

Working as an insurance agent, I learned the ins-and-outs of insurance, investing, estate, and legacy planning. By partnering with attorneys, I found myself continuing to question the law route while pursuing the financial realm. I could see the impact my work was having on families and real people. I was always focused on helping others, making a difference, running my own practice with my own clients, and not having a boss to report to each day.

PURPOSE IN THE PROFIT

Over the course of two years, I gained a good number of clients, but I was not happy with the results. I accumulated a lot of debt trying to cover my expenses during the first year, which added to my debt from college.

In 1996, I joined a mutual fund company where I called on financial advisors of major financial firms as an internal wholesaler. My role was to explain our investment products to financial advisors so they could determine if the investments would be appropriate for their clients. It was during my two-year stint at this financial company that my life shifted.

My grandmother, Estelle Wilken, was 84 at this time and her health began to decline. She went back and forth between her home, hospital, rehab center, my uncle's house, and eventually, a nursing home covered by Medicaid. Widowed longer than she was married, my grandmother worked before and after my grandfather's death. She worked to cover the bills, and she did not have the financial resources to save for later, which could have enabled her to have care in her own home. She passed away in January of 1997.

This was a turning point for me. I was disheartened that my grandmother was not able to save for her future. She did not have a resource to guide and help her. A trusted advisor could have helped her when she was widowed at age 56. I believe advice at that time could have enabled her to be in a better financial position as her health began to decline. This experience compelled me to educate women to be proactive about their finances, not reactive to a crisis, like a divorce or death. Growing up living paycheck to paycheck, I saw an opportunity with young professionals to teach them how to live below their means and save more, not spend more. This gave me a great sense of purpose.

I developed my presentation skills and public speaking became something I really enjoyed. I enrolled in a twelve-week Dale Carnegie course. Based upon the fundamentals of the book, *How to Win Friends and Influence People* authored by Dale Carnegie, I learned how to remember names and make genuine connections when meeting new people. At the end of the course, there was a presentation finale and I was selected the "Sales Talk Champion" by my classmates. I was stunned and honored to be recognized by a diverse group of professionals for my speech. This accomplishment, and the training I experienced, increased my confidence and I was ready for another career shift.

In May of 1998, I became an Edward Jones financial advisor and began to build relationships in my community. I literally went door-to-door introducing myself. Using the skills and the confidence of the Dale Carnegie training, I began to teach investment classes at the park district to educate people on investments and risk. It was an opportunity for the community to see me as an informative resource, and it created opportunities for business. Wanting to focus on women in particular, I hosted seminars for women, and I joined the Darien Women's Club and American Association of University Women, AAUW.

As I began meeting with potential clients, I took the time to get to know them personally and find out what was most important to them. I found out where they stood financially and how they got where they were, for better or worse. I wanted to know how they envisioned their retirement years and if they planned to fund one or more college educations. I shared my personal experience of having a role in funding my education, and I know my clients appreciated it. Clients shared ideas with me too, and I learned how they shifted responsibility to their kids to cover their first year of tuition so they would take it seriously and do the work.

When I set out to become a financial advisor, I knew I had the education and training to make a difference, but I underestimated the impact clients would have on me. Over time, I have become close with them and I feel like my older clients are adopted grandparents. Learning about a cancer diagnosis or seeing a client decline due to Alzheimer's is difficult, particularly when you regard them more as friends or family. Visiting clients in the hospital, at home after surgery, or paying respects at a funeral are all things I do because I care about them, and I know they care about me too. When I got married in 2014, I was overwhelmed by the cards, flowers, and gifts I received from clients for my wedding. One of my 90-year-old clients sent me flowers with a note that said, "Congratulations on your new merger." I was genuinely touched by his kindness and caring.

CHANGE AND CHALLENGE

During my first ten years as a financial advisor, I worked through two significant stock market downturns. The first was during the September 11th terrorist attacks, and the second was the great recession. I was responsible for providing frequent communication and education to my clients during these challenging times.

Clients and I would meet and discuss their long-term goals, and I would share the outlook of the economy and the markets. I sought advice from more experienced advisors, I continued to teach classes about investing, and maintained my client base. There were good days, bad days and very long days.

Naturally, people will worry when their portfolio declines in value. I had to learn how to differentiate between logic and emotion. I would tackle their concerns head on and address them. We were in this together. When the markets were up again, clients felt better about their portfolio value. I continued to reiterate that market fluctuation is normal, so they could prepare for the next time. Clients trusted me, and I took it to heart.

It was during this tumultuous time that I decided to train for the Chicago marathon, which I thought could help me manage my stress. Back then, I was completely inactive. But I had met a friend during a three-day breast cancer walk who inspired me to undertake the training to complete the 26.2 mile run. Training helped me prioritize my work and my time. I ran early mornings before work, and I ran long runs with a group on Saturday mornings. I felt calmer, re-energized, and more focused. I not only completed my first marathon in 2000, but I went on to complete six more. While I trained, I got fit, ate better, managed stress, and created a new circle of friends. I was inspired and wanted to inspire others too.

During the fall of 2013, I had an unexpected challenge due to family health issues. My dad had been hospitalized and while undergoing a stress test, he flatlined and went into cardiac arrest. They shocked him, did chest compressions, and thankfully, they revived him. I got the call to come to the hospital, and as I arrived, he was being wheeled away to have three stents put in his heart. Two days later, he had a defibrillator surgically implanted.

Meanwhile, my mom had been ill since she had stomach surgery in the summer, and she was not doing well. She was now in the same hospital as my dad. As if this were not enough, my fiancé, now husband, Enrique, was diagnosed with pleural effusion as a result of pneumonia. Enrique was hospitalized now too, about an hour from my parents, and he needed surgery by a cardiothoracic surgeon to handle this infection gone awry.

It was during this time that I felt the love and compassion of my friends, family, clients, and colleagues. I had support from everywhere. My brother flew in from Washington state. Coworkers made home-cooked meals and dropped them off at my home. Friends came to one hospital and took needed family items over to the other hospital. Clients were understanding when I needed to reschedule appointments and were surprised when I came into the office to get work done. I received notes and flowers, and people were constantly checking in to see if they could help. All three of my loved ones-- my dad, my mom, and Enrique-- made it through.

Enrique had the most difficult surgery and recovery. He was sent home needing to have an IV every day for a month, and it was my responsibility to administer it. Balancing family health issues with day-to-day work and doctor appointments, I simply could not manage this on my own and am forever grateful to everyone who helped.

DOING THINGS DIFFERENTLY

Early on in my career, I felt I could do things "my way," but I usually ended up rocking the boat. I was often told that coming into a situation like a bull in a china shop was not the way to effectively get things done and build lifelong relationships. I was praised, and simultaneously cautioned, for my direct communication. Looking for challenges and being results-oriented, I was hungry for success and achievement and so I adopted a lifelong learning mentality.

It was incumbent on me to learn and seek out resources to adapt and grow as a professional and as a leader. I learned a lot through experience, executing the day-to-day activity. An avid reader, I found books and articles to be of tremendous value in furthering my knowledge and creating new experiences. I hired a business coach and took additional classes so I could expand my views and surround myself with like-minded people.

Looking back on my first years in business, there were times where I felt like a small step up the ladder was a big win. Many times, I stepped down a few rungs to reassess and begin again. Occasionally, I found I did not set my goal high enough so I would reevaluate and aim higher. Even when I was super excited about a new goal or endeavor, I would imagine an arduous climb and get bogged down with worry and stress. I learned I could accomplish things on my own, but mostly, I learned how to reach out for advice, help, and encouragement so I had support to see me through.

There have been people whose shoulders I stood on as they mentored, motivated, and challenged me and my thinking. Their words and feedback influenced how I approached my goals and how I stayed motivated to achieve success. Although they were my goals, once I shared them, I felt we were in them together. That inspired me to be more intentional in elevating others on their climb to the top.

After 20 years of building a successful practice and taking on leadership roles within the firm, I recently became a regional leader. I am now responsible for more than 70 financial advisors and branch teams. I am as excited about the opportunity to learn as I am for the opportunity to lead. As I continue to climb my ladder, I am thrilled to help others climb, and in some cases, even build their own ladder of success.

Each of us has an opportunity to give, whether it be our

time, advice, direction, or inspiration. I hope you learn from me and my experience that one small gesture can be significant to another person. Be intentional. When you see a person climbing the steps of life's ladder, influence them to keep climbing. Give to them and they will be empowered to give to others. Rest assured your influence will make an impact.

MENTORSHIP MOMENT

Here's two important concepts that have helped me in my growth as an entrepreneur.

1. **Find the Right "One."** It's invaluable to have someone you can turn to for frank, ongoing advice and support about your ideas and goals. It can be a good friend, spouse, peer, or business associate, but they should be able to be honest with you when something is awesome but also be able to talk you off a ledge. The more deeply they know you, the more they can guide you, and the more wholeheartedly authentic and vulnerable you can be with them.

2. **Slow down to speed up!** This has become my mantra to make sure I am not just being busy, but productive. It means to first slow down and evaluate where I am today and what I'm doing with my day, week, or month. Is my work truly leading to the results I want? Or am I just exhausting myself? When I slow down, I can see what's most important and prioritize, delegate, or remove anything not contributing to my goal. Once I'm clear on my direction, I create a plan to get back on track.

Then I speed up by implementing the plan, and now I can

do it with enthusiasm and renewed energy because I've had that moment of pause. I keep track of the things I said I would do, and I ask my peers to hold me accountable as needed.

It works to "slow down to speed up!"

BIOGRAPHY

Jennifer Wilken is a financial advisor who joined Edward Jones in 1998 and understands that the key to building long-term relationships is educating clients to make decisions with long-lasting benefits. Jennifer has more than 25 years in the financial industry and often works generationally to create financial strategies for grandparents, adult children, and grandchildren.

Jennifer has served the community as a past board member of the Darien Chamber of Commerce, the American Association of University Women and the Benedictine University Women's Leadership Council. She was named the 2018 "Woman of

Influence" from Chicago Business Journal and was a nominee for the Young Entrepreneurial award by Athena International.

She is a graduate of Southern Illinois University with a BA in Political Science and has earned the professional designation of AAMS® (Accredited Asset Management Specialist) for individuals who commit to a code of ethics and agree to pursue continuing education. At Edward Jones she has volunteered as a mentor, field trainer, coach, keynote speaker, recruiting leader and a WINGS leader (women's initiative for new growth strategies).

Jennifer has completed seven marathons. She is married to Enrique and has two children, Sofia and Andres, and Lucia, a border collie, and Ellie, a Great Pyrenees.

Jennifer Wilken

jennifer.wilken@edwardjones.com

(630) 435-5433

LinkedIn: /jennifer-wilken-792a036

MY VELVETEEN YEARS: HOW I BECAME A "REAL" LEADER

—

Amy Wasson-Throw

"We are humans first and leaders second."

This is a story of my evolution as a leader and the formative challenges that I encountered along the way. It's a tale of deep personal growth through connection with appropriate vulnerability that's made me the leader I am today. It's one leader's journey from natural confidence and leadership abilities through a life that presented challenges that rocked her foundation, challenged her concept of vulnerability, and allowed her to think, see, feel differently, and emerge as a thoughtful and graceful leader. In essence, it's about the shift from success to significance. As I have discovered, true leadership is always other-focused.

As you read my story, I encourage you to think about your own leadership journey. Voltaire said, "Judge a man by his questions, rather than his answers." What were your most formative experiences in becoming a leader and how have they shaped who you are today? In your opinion, what are the most important characteristics of a wise leader?

In the classic children's book, *The Velveteen Rabbit*, a young boy receives a new stuffed toy rabbit for Christmas. The Velveteen Rabbit lives in the nursery with all of the other toys, waiting for the day when the Boy will choose him for play. While waiting, the Rabbit befriends a tattered Skin Horse, the wisest resident of the nursery, who reveals the goal of all nursery toys: to be made "real" through the love of a child. "'Real isn't how you are made," says the Horse. "It's a thing that happens to you. When a child loves you for a long, long, time, not just to play with, but REALLY loves you, then you become "Real." Once you are "Real," you can't become unreal again. It lasts for always."

In many ways, I've been a leader since I was a child. I'm the oldest of four children with an outgoing, task-oriented personality. I'm focused on solving problems and getting results, balanced with an ability to influence and inspire others, interact with people, and create excitement about projects and passions. According to various personality assessments, including the DISC and Strengthsfinder, my love for learning, ability to set my mind to something and achieve it, and my talent for activating others and communicating effectively all contribute to my identity as a leader.

DISCOVERING LEADERSHIP

I was raised in a loving home with a great mix of firm boundaries, love, and the benefit of natural consequences when I made poor choices. As a result, I developed the ability to learn lessons from my mistakes early in my life, no matter what the situation or challenge.

I have memories of "leading others" as far back as fourth grade when I would organize activities with my cousin, Susan. We were both into all things "horsey," and I would plan hours of organized play as we created infinite adventures and lives for our toy horses. As I look back, there was always a purpose in everything I did, even in play. During my high school years, I led various extracurricular activities was senior class president, and was also involved in leadership in my church youth group.

For the most part, I've been confident in who I am and my ability to accomplish things and succeed. I naturally lean towards taking charge of situations, paving roads, and getting others to join me in the pursuit of a common goal. In high school, college, and early in my career, I was often thought to be older because of my maturity level and presence.

Early in my professional career, I was quickly promoted from an entry-level job to a branch manager position with responsibility for profit and loss and a team of peers and people older than me. Making the shift from peer to leader wasn't easy. I had to learn the art of being relational, friendly, and simultaneously firm when it came to office practices. I began to learn the importance of managing my thoughts and emotions as a leader in order to stay grounded and calm during times of drama in the office.

At the ripe age of 26, I took a job as an outplacement consultant for mid to senior-level executives. I found myself giving career counsel to individuals who were 20 to 30 years older than me. I was continually rewarded and praised for being strong, confident, capable and "a leader," and therefore I was continually developed and promoted in my corporate jobs.

These experiences shaped my belief that strength, confidence, and the ability to get things done were important parts of leadership. While I did feel confident much of the time, I also had a deep hidden urge to appear polished, productive, and look like I had it "all together." Even when I was unsure of myself, as we all are sometimes, it was hard to be vulnerable and ask people for help. It wasn't until later in life that I recognized that my constant, internal battle to be able to do things well the first time sometimes robbed me of the joy of "being a beginner" and the process of learning through mistakes and failures.

At times, this inner drive to do it all well produced an illusion that I had it all together. Of course, no human being has it all together, but others are less likely to open up about their own insecurities and struggles with someone who appears confident and strong. And as I was to discover, leaders must be able to connect on a human level with the people they lead.

My first inkling that there was more to leadership than confidence, strength, and capability came in college. The resident director of my dorm and many close friends encouraged me to apply for a coveted position of Resident Assistant (RA). The RA lives on a college dorm floor and is responsible for developing relationships with students, supporting them during difficult times, organizing social events, and supporting spiritual development. It was a highly regarded leadership position and my friends all told me I'd be a perfect RA. Based on my extensive leadership experience in high school, my outgoing personality, my desire to help others and my confident, capable persona, I had a strong feeling I would be selected. I applied and interviewed, leaving the meeting with high hopes of becoming an RA and helping the women on my floor the following year. A week later, I got the devastating news that I didn't get the job. I was astonished, confused, hurt, and embarrassed. I couldn't understand why this strong confident woman (me) didn't get picked.

Eventually, I learned the reason. The student life committee thought I was too confident, too strong, and too put together! They feared that other students wouldn't be comfortable coming to me with their problems, that I might not be able to relate to people, and that students wouldn't open up to me. WOW… I was dumbfounded and baffled. How could I face the friends who'd encouraged me to apply? I simply couldn't understand how my greatest strength could be viewed as a weakness. My beliefs about what makes a good leader were shattered and for the first time in my adult life, I was unsure about myself. How could I be a good leader in the future if being strong and confident would work against me? I now understand that this painful, confusing, and life-altering experience was the first step on my journey to becoming a real leader. The seeds of growing into a full circle leader of significance were planted in that moment.

BECOMING REAL

In 1994, I stepped off my successful career track to start a family and raise three sons. I poured my interest and abilities into volunteer roles at church. Again, I became a leader and was praised for my competence, capability, strength, and organizational skills.

After a very rigorous interview process with my women's ministry group, I was invited to lead a group of women on a weekly basis. I believed I was leading well, but as I look back on those years, I realize that I had much to learn about real leadership.

Yes, I was able to listen to other's challenges and struggles, empathize with them, and even give advice and direction. But now I understand that it was very hard for me to open up about my own struggles as I related to these women. I thought it was my job to be strong for them, but it would have been more meaningful and significant if I'd been able to be real and vulnerable with them. I would have been a better leader if I had shared my very self with them, not just my listening ear and advice. I now have learned that the path to human connection comes through vulnerability.

My second step on the journey to becoming "real" happened in 2000. After the birth of my third son, I experienced postpartum depression which developed into clinical depression, hospitalization, and counseling on and off for a period of 12 years. When I was first hospitalized, my church friends who knew me as ministry leader couldn't understand my depression. I appeared so strong and confident!

The experience shook me to my core. The confidence and strength that I had been praised for most of my life had completely disappeared. I could barely get through the day taking care of my three sons. I constantly felt scattered, hopeless, and unable to contribute to anything in a meaningful way. The journey through depression leveled me AND it also started to refine me.

During those years, I was forced to ask for help from friends, family, and professionals. I felt weak, hopeless, and worthless. I questioned my ability to be a good mom. I felt like someone had placed a thick, heavy, wet, wool blanket over me and I would never get out from under it. But to my surprise, as I began to ask for help and share my needs and deepest feelings, my relationships with friends and family deepened. The more I opened up about my needs, my relationships grew richer and more profound. Every day, I prayed that I would be able to encourage others in meaningful ways in the future as a result of my experience.

Fast forward to 2004. After an eight-year professional hiatus, I was starting to climb out of depression. God dropped an opportunity into my life, and I launched my own business as an image and style consultant with the international fashion brand, cabi. Through this business, I hoped to encourage women "from the outside in."

I found that my journey with depression and my desire to be changed through it had given me an ability to see below the surface. I could now sense when others were struggling, and I could journey alongside them with true encouragement when appropriate. This business became a lifeline for me, a mission, and a huge success.

During the course of my 15-year career with cabi, I worked hard and smart to achieve sales goals. After two short years working part-time, I achieved the $100,000 sales circle that represented the top three percent of the company. I was invited to serve on an executive leadership advisory group and expanded my business to a team of 18 women across the country. I led, coached, and trained them.

I had a dream to become the top sales person, and in 2014, I achieved that dream. I ranked number one out of 3,800 sales people and broke all previous sales records. I was considered a success, admired by many, and often called upon to teach at national conferences. People sought me out for advice on how to grow their business. In the world's eyes, I was a successful leader.

As my team of women expanded, I found myself spending more time trying to help them become successful in their own businesses. In countless conversations, I tried to lead them by sharing my success strategies and suggesting things I had done that would help them grow their own business. To me, it seemed straightforward: "Follow my success strategies and you will be successful. If I can do it, so can you." But when some continued to feel unsuccessful, I once again hit a "leadership wall." I felt like a failure as a leader and knew my approach wasn't working. Once more, my strengths and personal success seemed to be working against me.

Enter my first coach who helped me understand that what my team needed from me was less advice, fewer suggestions, and more listening and understanding their unique strengths and dreams for their business. They needed to know I had a true, deep interest in them as human beings.

As I started to truly focus on others and get curious about their deepest fears, hopes, and dreams for their business, things started to change. I began each meeting with an intention of asking open ended questions and simply listening to them. I asked questions about their families, what was bringing them joy, and what was keeping them up at night. I focused less on the business and more on personal connection and building a relationship.

My interactions improved and I became a better listener. I sought first to understand them and be present to them as human beings, not just a leader relating to a subordinate. Soon my team members started achieving their goals. I felt like I was becoming a better, more effective, and empowering leader who could help others reach their own potential and business goals.

VELVETEEN YEARS

Then in August 2014, a month after achieving the top sales award out of 3,800 people, the bottom fell out of my personal life and things changed dramatically in my work relationships. My marriage, which had been struggling the past four years, was on the brink of ending. I had spiraled into high anxiety and periods of behavior that were uncharacteristically hyperactive. I felt completely overwhelmed. I was in such a bad state just trying to survive the stress at home that I became extremely self-focused.

My behavior became hurtful to my family at home and my colleagues and team members at work. Some of the relationships that I had worked so hard to build with my team were shattered. My teammates were asking to be led by someone else, and I was encouraged to quietly pull back from the executive leadership committee. My leader took over my team and lovingly shielded me from the negativity. It was so kind of her, but at the time, I was self-conscious, humiliated, and worried. How would I ever recover? Would I ever be able to lead again? And did I have what it took to repair and restore those relationships within my team?

I lovingly call these years of feeling lost and overwhelmed my "Velveteen Rabbit" years. My years of depression and anxiety and the consequences of my actions were the years that made me more "real." Yes, the love of others also helped me become real, as did the destruction of all that I held as important. When it all fell away, I became tattered and real, like the Skin Horse. These experiences helped me grow in wisdom, depth, and understanding of myself and others.

I'm grateful to say that four years later, through anxiety therapy counseling and a diligent commitment to healing and rebuilding relationships, my marriage is intact and so are my relationships at work. I'm on the path to becoming the leader that I always wanted to be: a leader who is truly other-focused, curious, and who seeks to first understand and open doors for others. I have finally become a real leader: authentic, accessible, and genuine.

It took my velveteen years to teach me that true leadership is not about your success. True leadership is about being "real," listening deeply, infusing others with strategic encouragement, shining a light on their strengths, and helping them soar and succeed in a way that's uniquely theirs. True leadership is the subtle and powerful shift from success to significance. True leadership is always others focused.

It took a series of breakdowns to learn these lessons, but I chose to use the breakdowns to achieve breakthroughs. Breakthroughs are possible when we are willing to surrender to the pain, glean life lessons from it and seek change from the inside out rather than expecting others or circumstances to change for us. These difficult and painful life experiences have truly enabled me to lead in a way that is authentic and gracious, other-focused and strategically encouraging...in other words..."real."

The pain of my mental illness and personal crisis helps me now lead with my humanity, vulnerability, and strength to understand others and give them what they need.

We each bring our full self to work each day, including our

strengths and shadows, good and bad, joy and pain, hopes and fears. This I know for sure: to lead with significance, we must be deeply committed to knowing and understanding people first as human beings. Know what makes them tick, where they flourish, and where they're likely to fall.

The process of being coached and coaching others in their businesses inspired me to launch my own coaching and consulting firm in 2017. I now help leaders in corporate America, entrepreneurs, and small business owners as they face the day-to-day challenges of leading others in significant and authentic ways. My unique gift in this endeavor is helping each client get to the root of what's blocking their progress, whether it's professional or personal.

Had I known then what I know now, I bet I would have gotten that RA job. My velveteen rabbit years helped me understand that we are humans first and leaders second, and that there's always emotion and a human element at the base of every challenge we face whether it's our own challenges or challenges with others. Now, I'm equipped to help other leaders see through a different lens, guiding them to first develop relationships with the people they lead and to create personal connections before they ask for performance. These are the indispensable steps in the shift from success to significance and becoming a leader who is other-focused.

In other words…a "real" leader!

MENTORSHIP MOMENT

Think about how you show up as a leader naturally and how your vulnerability can help you connect on a deeper level with the amazing people you lead.

These seven principles pave the way for the "human connection"- not boss to employee, but human to human. When you let others in and connect with them in an authentic way, they will become more open with you and a beautiful collision of human connection will imbue the work and success of everyone involved.

Reflect on and choose two of these top seven practices for significant leadership to begin practicing this week:

1. Remember, it's not about you.

2. Seek first to understand.

3. Listen deeply with your body, not just your ears.

4. Stay curious.

5. Your goal is helping team members achieve. Look for ways to put the spotlight on them.

6. Help them grow into their crowns.

7. Master the art of "appropriate vulnerability." Let them see your softer side and be open about your struggles.

Answer and reflect....

1. What do you believe are the five essential qualities of a significant leader? Could you be wrong?

2. What is the biggest internal obstacle in your leadership life? What would overcoming it do for you and your leadership relationships?

3. Who is one person that needs your authenticity and deep listening as a leader and how could this change your relationship?

4. What is one thing you'll do differently as a result of reading this chapter, and who will hold you accountable for action?

BIOGRAPHY

Amy Wasson Throw is an award-winning entrepreneur, executive coach, and speaker. She is the creator of the Full Circle 7 approach to executive presence and leadership, which helps people become powerful, respected leaders who are admired and trusted by others. With her guidance, smart and successful women successfully navigate the difficult shift from tactical to strategic and self-focused to others-focused to navigate the unwritten politics in their organizations.

A sought-after speaker and facilitator, Amy's engaging approach both educates and entertains. Full of lessons gleaned from her experiences in both corporate and small business environments and 15 years as a successful entrepreneur, she's known for her straight talk, wisdom, and tips on "handling the human element" along with a healthy dose of strategic encouragement. Her clients describe her as Authentic,

Encouraging, Insightful, Curious and Strategic.

Amy offers complimentary coaching conversations for people who are ready for a change from to uncertainty to confidence, informant to influencer, manager to executive and executive to visionary. She helps clients ditch confusion and get clarity, lose uncertainty and get confidence, stop feeling alone as a leader and gain a strategic thinking partner. When potential and performance collide, she's the catalyst for transformation.

Amy Wasson-Throw
www.amythrow.com
(773) 570-3073
Facebook/Instagram: @amythrowgroup

LEADING BEYOND SUCCESS

Brian Marshall

"As leaders, we must model the behaviors that we expect in others."

I married my high school sweetheart in 1982, just six months after graduating from high school. While we were excited for our future, very few people believed our marriage would last. I was determined to prove them wrong by being the best husband, father, and leader of our family that I could be. This is when I first realized that proving others wrong would be the fuel driving me to push harder at things in my life; I was driven to be successful and I was not going to let anybody or anything get in my way. I was determined to prove to the world they were wrong.

I also learned my first big leadership lesson. Great leaders find their motivation from within and have an unshakable belief in their ability to succeed, even when the odds are against them.

CRASHES AND AFTERMATHS

The experience of getting married at 18, becoming a dad at 19, and starting my first business by the age of 21 shaped my work ethic and sparked my passion to be successful in life and in business. From 1985 to 2001, I started a number of companies, was part of a leadership team of a publicly-traded technology company, and in 2000, I became an officer with one of the hottest pre-IPO tech start-ups in the country. These experiences had a profound influence on the type of leader I would become. I was a "follow me, do as I do, lead by example" type of leader. I was primarily focused on results and my own personal success.

In 2001, I left the tech start-up and decided to take a five-year break from business to spend more time at home with family. From the outside looking in, I appeared to have it all-- big house, expensive cars, perfect family, lots of money in the bank, etc. From the inside looking out, 2001 to 2009 were actually the most difficult years of my life. It was the struggle to get through those years that had a profound impact on me, and ultimately shaped who I am today.

In February 2002, my oldest daughter was in a serious car accident. This event was a wake-up call causing me to realize that I had been focusing on the wrong things in life. True, I had chosen to focus on success up until then and decided to take time off to spend with family. However, without work to do, I found myself lost. I struggled with my sense of purpose and my endless "prove them wrong" energy had dwindled. I realized that I had finally achieved success and could not stop wondering if this was all there was to life.

I was not as happy as I thought I would be. I lost the sense of purpose that drove me up to this point, and I felt betrayed and angry that life was not as I thought it would be once I achieved "success." Yet, there was a gift in all of this: I began to look beyond success. Unfortunately, though, things got worse before they got better.

In 2007, my financial world came crashing down around me. I was investing heavily in real estate beginning in 2001 and had accumulated a significant portfolio of residential properties from 2001-07. Everything was great until it wasn't. The first shoe to drop was in early 2007, with the collapse of the subprime lending market. By 2008, we were in a full- blown economic meltdown, which triggered a catastrophic failure of my real estate business. By the end of 2008, I had to shut down my business and was forced into personal bankruptcy. This was one of the most difficult periods in my life. I worked for 20+ years and sacrificed so much to achieve "success," only to watch it all disappear in what felt like the blink of an eye.

Later, I was able to view those years as one of the greatest gifts of my life. I came out of that traumatic financial experience with a laser-sharp focus on what was most important. This humbling experience allowed me to look at life from a different perspective--one from which I began to put the needs of others ahead of my own. It changed me to the core of my being and I emerged from this experience as a different leader than I had been in the past. I became a Servant Leader, focused on creating significance by serving others.

TRANSFORMATION AND GROWTH

In 2010, I started a financial services business in Chicago. My desire was to help other business leaders so they would never have to go through the financial crisis that I had just experienced. I truly wanted to serve others and use my story to help motivate and inspire them to begin thinking beyond success. It was troubling to me that you could sacrifice so much and achieve success, only to watch it disappear like it did for so many of us in 2008. It turns out, in hindsight, that this was my third attempt to build a business around serving others. While the third time was not the charm, it is a part of the journey that has shaped me into the leader that I am today.

I decided to walk away from a very successful financial services startup at the end of 2013. I was back to making lots of money, working too much, and feeling totally unfulfilled in life. I was doing it to myself again. After lots of reflection, I decided to follow my gut and go in a direction that was completely different than anything I had done previously. I was determined to discover my purpose in life and make it my mission. You could say I took a "leap of faith."

In mid-2013 I conceived the idea for a new type of business and founded Transformational Growth Partners in January 2014. I was not yet sure if there was even a market for the work I would do or what people would be willing to invest in themselves for my services. Fortunately, it didn't take long to find out that the marketplace was in desperate need of Transformational Growth Partners.

I often get asked what we do. My answer these days is simple: we help build high- performance teams that consistently produce great results. It doesn't matter whether these teams are looking to win a national championship, dominate their respective marketplace, or change the world by helping others. As long as there are people looking to work together to produce amazing results, we can help them get there. You see, it all comes down to leadership, or more specifically, "vulnerability-based leadership." The best leaders consistently lead organizations that produce great results.

The one common denominator I've found within these great organizations is that their leaders focus not on the results themselves, but instead on the behaviors that are responsible for producing great results. They deal with the natural dysfunctions that occur when people work together in teams. What I have found most fascinating is that great leaders make their teams stronger by leading from behind, from a place of service. They see their role from a completely different perspective than that of a traditional leader. What follows is my attempt to break down the key success factors that I've witnessed along the course of my experience working with high-performance teams who have dared to go beyond success.

HIGH PERFORMANCE SUCCESS

Over the years I've become obsessed with studying the concept of "High Performance (HP) Teamwork." I'll admit, I'm a total geek when it comes to this stuff. There is something magical about watching these teams work, and witnessing the results they produce over and over again. What's really interesting though, is that they make it look easy, and they seem to be having fun in the process.

I've discovered that the first and most important responsibility of leadership is to create a safe environment where each member of their team can speak "their truth," which is often times different than "your truth" or "the truth," but I digress. You see, people have a need to be heard and understood. When a leader creates a safe space for team members to openly share their thoughts and feelings, and those team members respond by getting vulnerable and sharing, the team begins to trust each other more and more.

Leaders of HP teams must model this behavior by going first and being vulnerable in front of the team. Not once or twice, but all of the time. Doing so sends a message to the rest of the team that it's ok to speak "your truth." They live by a pragmatic motto. Admit you screwed up, learn from it, and let it go. In short, great leaders create "trust" through vulnerability. They share their failures with the same enthusiasm as they share their victories. In doing so, they are modeling the behavior they expect from the rest of the team members they are leading.

High Performance teams are built on a foundation of trust. It is the primary function of leadership to build and maintain that trust-based environment so that it becomes ingrained in the culture of their organizations and owned by each and every member of the team from the lowest levels of the organization to the very top.

Once the environment of trust is established, team members can engage in healthy debate around critical decisions that need to be made while tapping into the collective mindset of the team. When this is accomplished, the ideas transcend those of the individual and become the product of the collective mindset of those involved. This process is commonly referred to as brainstorming. It gives a voice to everyone involved in the process so that we all feel heard and understood without judgement. It is the role of the leader to maintain and protect the safety of the environment for this to become a sustainable process.

The first time I witnessed this in action was in Silicon Valley with the tech startup. This passionate sharing of ideas between team members was the fuel that drove innovation in that company. Once I experienced this, I was hooked.

When the team engages in healthy brainstorming, the leader must make a decision on how to proceed. Often, there are conflicting viewpoints and ideas generated during the brainstorming process. It is the role of the leader to weigh the various options and make a decision to move forward. It is the role of the leader to communicate that decision clearly to all involved in the process. It is then the leader's job to get a firm commitment from each team member to do everything in their power to make the decision work, including those who argued against it in the brainstorming process. Once each team member makes a clear commitment to support the new decision, no one has the right to say, "I told you it wouldn't work."

Lastly, leaders are responsible for creating an environment of accountability around the commitments that the team has made. The most important aspect of this process is in maintaining an environment of integrity around agreements amongst team members, including the leaders. If a commitment is broken, it is the role of the leader to facilitate a process of cleaning up broken agreements. Each member of the team is ultimately responsible for maintaining their own integrity and owning their broken agreements. It is also the leader's role to facilitate when someone is out of integrity and not taking ownership of the choices that they made around the broken agreements.

FOUR KEY AREAS OF INTEGRITY

Integrity means to be aligned first within ourselves and then with others.

When you speak of leadership, there are four key areas of integrity that are essential for the team to embrace. When a team member is "out of integrity" in any of the four key areas, the level of trust that others have in them begins to diminish, ultimately creating dysfunction within the team. When a leader allows members of the team to continually be out of integrity, that leader's ability to lead becomes compromised. Great leaders hold themselves and their team members accountable for getting back, and staying in, integrity in the following key areas:

1. Emotional Awareness: This is the ability to be awake and aware of what you are feeling at the moment, be able to locate these feelings accurately in your body and communicate your feelings clearly so that others can understand them. Doing so creates clarity and builds trust through vulnerability.

2. Agreements: Be clear about what you want and don't want. Do not make agreements that you do not want to make and keep the agreements that you do make. You may need to re-negotiate and clean up broken agreements. Own the outcome of your broken agreement and work to get back into integrity immediately. Doing so creates deeper trust and lets others know they can depend on you to keep your commitments.

3. Communication: Be an authentic listener and speaker. Listen with undivided attention and listen for accuracy, understanding, emotions, and exactly what the team member wants. As an authentic speaker you must take responsibility for communication until it is clear that the other person understands. Don't assume that what you are saying is clear. Ask them to repeat back what you have said to confirm that they heard and understand you. Doing this will create greater clarity and help avoid disconnects within the team.

4. Responsibility: Take full responsibility for the circumstance in your life and actively promote and inspire 100 percent responsibility in others. In other words, stop making excuses and own the choices you make and the consequences they produce. Doing this builds deep bonds of trust between team members. All members of the team must be held to the same standards of integrity, especially the leaders. Vulnerable leaders will turn themselves in when they are out of integrity, even for the smallest of infractions. As leaders, we must model the behaviors that we expect in others. We must shift from defensiveness, excuses, and blame to seeking the truth and holding each other accountable.

Once an organization is able to implement each of the disciplines in this model, the byproduct is a team that consistently produces great results. In other words, you will get the results you desire by focusing on the disciplines I have outlined.

While it might be tempting to attempt to do this on your own, my advice would be to seek out someone with experience and expertise in having done this before. I learned this lesson the hard way earlier in my career when I tried to implement this structure for a company I owned. It turned out that I was a big part of the problem but failed to recognize it. While I learned a lot from the experience, it was an expensive lesson. Failure can be a great teacher, but I've made it my mission to help others learn from my failures so that they can benefit from my experience without the pain and suffering involved in personally failing themselves.

Today I am living my mission: "To motivate, mentor, and inspire others to be great servant leaders." I do this through the work I am doing in my business, Transformational Growth Partners, and through such great non-profit organizations as "The Crucible Project" (www.thecrucibleproject.org) and "Battle Cry International" (www.battlecryinternational.org).

These organizations and their volunteers are helping to transform lives and build strong leaders by using Jesus Christ as the model for great leadership.

I wish you great success in your life journey and encourage you to press on through the tough times and stop to enjoy the good times. Remember, don't get so busy building a successful career that you forget to live a significant life.

MENTORSHIP MOMENT

Integrity Inventory Exercise: I constantly challenge leaders to step into the four areas of integrity I outline in this chapter. If you are interested in becoming a stronger, more effective leader, I encourage you to take an integrity inventory of the agreements in your life as a way to clean up and renegotiate the broken agreements that are undermining your leadership. You can start this process by doing the following exercise.

Step 1: INTEGRITY INVENTORY AROUND AGREEMENTS WITH OTHERS

Go through the list below and answer these two questions for each person/people in your life:

1. Have I kept all my agreements with them?
2. What agreement did I make that I haven't kept?
   - My Co-Workers
   - My Spouse
   - My Children
   - My Extended Family
   - Friends

Step 2: INTEGRITY INVENTORY AROUND AGREEMENTS WITH MYSELF

Go through the following list and answer these two questions for each area:

1. Have I kept all my agreements with myself?
2. What agreement did I make that I haven't kept?
   - Pleasure
   - Money
   - Time
   - Things
   - Health

Step 3: LIVING IN INTEGRITY AROUND AGREEMENTS

1. What are you willing to do to clean up agreements you have made, but not kept (from your Integrity Inventory) in order to get back into integrity?
2. Identify one agreement that you haven't kept where you made the agreement even though you really didn't want to make it. Briefly describe what happened as a result. What will you do to get back into integrity around this broken agreement?
3. What new agreements do you want to make?
4. What person will you get to support you in getting back into integrity around your agreements? How will you have him/her support you?

BIOGRAPHY

Brian Marshall, serial entrepreneur and founder of Transformational Growth Partners (TGP), has three decades of experience producing dramatic business results for start-ups as well as small and mid-size companies in the manufacturing, professional services, high-technology and financial service industries.

Brian founded TGP in 2014, based on his desire to help others experience life beyond business and financial success. In 2011, Brian co-founded the Chicago-based, professional services and advanced planning firm, Momentum Strategic Advisors, and in 2006 he and a partner started Alliance for Strategic Advantage, a sales training and management consultancy.

Brian has held leadership positions responsible for all aspects of business operations in roles ranging from CEO, CIO, VP of Operations, and Sales Leadership. He has also founded multiple start-ups in the technology, consulting, and financial services sectors. He currently serves on several boards for companies in the Chicago area.

In his role as Chief Information Officer of a publicly traded company, Brian received an AITP Chicago "CIO of the Year" Award in 2000. Brian and Tawnya, his wife of more than thirty-six years, live on a private lake in a rural town near Chicago where they spend time with their four adult children, grandchildren and dogs.

Brian Marshall
bmarshall@yourtgp.com
815-791-1810
LinkedIn: /brianmarshall

SWIVEL TO SUCCEED: LEADING THROUGH DIVERSIFICATION

Jeff Kubas

"Always seek opportunities and possibilities for growth."

You've heard the saying, "the only thing you can count on is that everything will change." That's why it's important to manage change and "swivel" your thinking to gain perspective. Pivoting between markets, priorities, and client focus has produced some of my biggest leadership challenges and triumphs.

GROWTH AND GRIT

Newly married, my wife Leslie and I were trying to build

a nest egg. After talking to a trusted friend about our financial goals, we established a small cleaning services company to supplement our incomes. We acquired a few accounts fairly quickly. At first, we did most of the work ourselves and then hired some part-time employees to help, as I still worked my day job in public service and was pursuing an accelerated program in business management. After some time, I left my public service job. My experience owning and managing the cleaning company proved fruitful. It led to an offer as an operations manager for a sizeable janitorial company. I accepted.

While gaining valuable hands-on experience in running a large-scale operation, I met two men who purchased a manufacturing business. Their operation was ramping up, and they needed more staff for assembly and light industrial work but were anticipating ebbs and flows in production. They needed a flexible workforce to grow and shrink with the upturns and slow periods of their business. From my cleaning business and work in the sector, I knew many dependable professionals willing to jump at the chance to work in manufacturing. Recognizing an opportunity, I proposed a flexible staffing solution for the manufacturing duo. They accepted and became the first client of FlexiCorps, the company that Leslie and I opened in 1992.

When we started the business, we had three young children, and I was still working full time at the janitorial company and part time back in public service, so Leslie was the company engine. On many mornings, Leslie took the children along with their lunchboxes and books to a manufacturing plant for an early client meeting before school. With his older siblings in school, my youngest son would beg Leslie to take him to meetings at his favorite client, who made gelato and would give him a generous sample each time.

As we built the business, we were always open to possibilities, however, at the same time we were very careful with our promises. If we committed to an opportunity, we were confident we could do it or we would not take it on at all. We encountered two key opportunities that put this principal to the test, but the results ultimately launched us into even greater realms of possibility.

The first happened while I was out of town on a vendor visit for the company I was working for at the time. I was on a business trip in Manchester, Vermont, enjoying some Ben and Jerry's after my meeting, when Leslie called with an urgent, huge, client opportunity. It was a retail chain seeking staffing for their 30-location project throughout the Northeast and Midwest. We had dabbled in retail staffing, but could we do a big job? The teleconference meeting was set and together Leslie and I spoke to them and listened to what they needed. After hearing their needs, we determined that we could do the work for them. Once alone, we looked at each other with the same question going through our heads: how are we going to do this? But as we worked through it and formulated a plan, it wasn't long before we looked at each other and said, "We can do this."

The second key moment happened in 2005 with one of our manufacturing clients. They asked us to evaluate the needs of their plant in Mississippi, which was struggling in both profitability and productivity in large part because of their relationship with their staffing vendor. We gave them what became our standard promise in similar situations as we grew: we would only take on the project if we felt that we could do it better than the local sources. With that agreement, we headed down south and spent months researching and determining a strategy for them. In the end, we found we could make a difference, so we accepted the job. This was our first opportunity to open an office in another state and it was an exciting, refreshing challenge that also taught us a lot. Today we have a presence in many states, with offices in such places as El Paso and Clearwater, and we are pros at setting up satellite businesses when needed.

I always muse that you don't know what you don't know. Leslie and I were both naïve about what we were getting into, but the business climate in the '90s was much easier than it is today. Manufacturing was plentiful, and we were doing well. Back then, we had no real plans for rapid expansion, but the workload could have supported it. Had we "made hay when the sun shone" we would now be a larger company. But I was still at my day job and didn't quit my full-time position until 2001, just in time for the economic downturn.

For the business and the family, the early 2000's were troublesome. Manufacturing was in decline, and at the same time, we lost one of our largest clients after they were purchased. After years of success, Leslie and I were unable to take a paycheck. We were falling behind on our mortgage and wondered if we could provide for our kids.

DIVERSIFY AND CONQUER

I began to see a light at the end of the tunnel, after a dark period, and that light's name was diversification. By providing staffing services across industries, we could grow strategically and mitigate risk. A downturn in one sector would not sink the staffing needs of another.

I don't know if you call it business sense or gut instinct, but we decided to concentrate on administrative services. We had dabbled in placing clerical and administrative staff before, but the time was right to expand our efforts. We acquired a small clerical and administrative staffing firm. A couple of their recruiters joined our forces, and we learned from each other. Our manufacturing business stalled due to economic forces, but our clerical and administrative staffing services remained steady.

A few years later, another opportunity presented itself when the owner of an administrative firm connected us with another small manufacturing staffing company that was for sale. Even though it didn't diversify us, it did give us a larger footprint in the western Chicago suburbs as we purchased and absorbed the business into FlexiCorps.

Eventually we turned our attention to staffing for higher level positions and acquired a firm that places office and mid-level managers. We recently acquired Cemco, an IT staffing and high-end recruiting company, which closes the loop on the diversification of our staffing services.

Leadership also means spearheading innovation when something even better is needed to serve clients. An example of our innovation that has been tremendously well received by our clients is Wage Tracker, a self-developed, proprietary software service, which helps clients easily manage timekeeping and payroll with 24/7 access to reports.

These decisions have placed me at the head of Vertex Resource Group, which is a holding company for our three major businesses: Wage Solutions, FlexiCorps and Cemco. This power trio is designed to buoy us through economic turbulence by their concentrations in different market sections.

When I'm asked to comment on our growth or my position as leader, I strive to recognize opportunity where others may not. Sometimes, I see an opportunity and don't have all the answers, but I believe that's okay. There's nothing wrong with learning as you go as long as you are confident of the outcome. You may struggle today, but that just makes tomorrow easier.

RELATIONSHIPS MATTER

Growth is best achieved through partnerships. I strive for this with my clients, and I believe that's why many have been with us for years. The client-vendor relationship is fragile and must always be tended, or it can implode.

Case in point. One of our biggest challenges in growing and diversifying our business was the obvious one—money. We could get the money, but as anyone in business knows, all banks are not the same. Our first loan came from a local bank that my parents had patronized for years. We worked well together for a while, but eventually, they could no longer accommodate us.

We moved to a larger, national chain bank and it was one of the biggest mistakes we ever made.

The deal up front was great. Interest rates were low, and we were given a bigger line of credit. But when the economy collapsed, our big bank was given a government bail-out. Shortly after, our line of credit expired. The bank gave us a document, explaining that they were going to cut our credit line and increase the interest rate to 13 percent, an incredible hike. Needless to say, I was shocked and irate. Our loan was never an underperformer, and we never missed a payment.

Because we were in a position to push back, we did. I refused to sign the document and pointed out the hypocrisy of treating small businesses this way after they had just accepted help from the government. Months later, they came back to us with a better rate but capped our line at the amount we had open. My hands were tied and there was no more I could do. If I had known this was the way we would be treated, I never would have chosen that bank.   Needless to say, we were with a new bank within a few months.

I share this story to illustrate the importance of the client relationship and also as advice to any small business owner in growth mode: carefully choose your banking institution. Because the big bank was more concerned with larger entities than our little company, we left. Had our relationship been handled better, the national bank may still have our business.

A DIFFERENT WAY

With experience, comes wisdom. Like most entrepreneurs, we've honed what we do through experience. Through encountering challenges and building upon successes, we have developed an effective system to best serve all people involved in the staffing process.

The image that comes to mind when people think of staffing firms is a storefront or strip mall with a sign encouraging job seekers to stop in and complete an application. Job placements are made on a first come, first serve basis in whatever openings are available that day. The staffing firm's need is the driving force behind the placement. If an administrative assistant is needed, and a retail customer service expert who knows Excel walks in, they may try to place that person behind a desk, wasting their valuable people skills and risking an unsatisfactory outcome.

Through experience, we've developed a better approach to staffing. We don't rely on public visibility and people dropping into our office. Instead, we recruit people into our office and find them a suitable position. All applicants, from the engineer to the box packer, go through the same extensive application process, from an initial phone screen, followed by an in-depth interview, to a thorough assessment of skills, strengths, work styles and goals. After we get to know our applicants, we place them in a position based on what is most important to them.

As a leader, it's my job to make sure the values set forth by my company are exhibited through the work we do, especially in dealing with our clients and candidates. The best way I've found to do this is through an example of hard work and of course, tending the relationships between our clients and candidates. From day one, I preached to our staff that we have two clients to serve: the clients that pay us and our job candidates. Job candidates deserve equal respect because they represent our company.

To show our respect, we give every candidate a transparent rundown of the pros and cons of the position before they accept. We try to draw them a realistic, no-holds-barred picture of what they will encounter. In fact, we want to get the candidate to say no to the position rather than accept a job they may not like, because we would rather have them be honest with us than show up at the position, become unhappy, and leave before the assignment is completed. If they know the negatives going in and still accept the position, they will be more likely to be happy there. Then they will continue to represent us well, the client will be happy, and the candidate will continue finding satisfying positions with us.

We also tell candidates that if they find they don't like their placement, they should tell us. If we understand what is unsatisfactory, we can replace them and/or find them a new position that is a better fit. This keeps candidates from walking out or not showing up. When our candidates are hired by our clients, that's a win for everybody and my model of success.

This system has helped us build loyal, happy clients and candidates who enjoy going to their jobs. Yes, for a small firm our process is surprisingly lengthy (usually more than ninety minutes), but we are looking to provide quality (not quantity) placements, and that is what our clients have come to expect from us.

When the wolf is at the door, it is hard to be principled. When you need the business, it is difficult to say no, even if the client is not a right fit for your company. It's hard to walk away from clients who don't "get us," but in the long run it leads to better clients and opens you up for future growth and diversity. This is especially true in the staffing industry, and it is easy to see how firms that attempt to place square pegs in round holes actually degrade the reputation of our profession and contribute to a dissatisfied marketplace.

As a leader, I've found that if you treat people well, they will perform well. We actively seek clients who are like-minded and appreciate how we do business. We know that candidates that are treated with respect will work harder and be happier overall. Clients who appreciate our approach treat us as a partner, not a commodity. When we feel appreciated, we work harder and so do our candidates.

I don't know what the future holds for our staffing company, but I'm also no longer naïve enough to believe things will stay the same for long. With an eye on the future, I'm ever ready to swivel, confident that with our solid foundation and experience in weathering storms we can do whatever we need to in order stay at the top of our game.

MENTORSHIP MOMENT

With my children working in the family business, they tend to hear my business philosophies repeated throughout their work week. Here are some of their "favorites:"

1. Sometimes we are our own worst enemy.

When we come up with an idea, often the next thought is how unrealistic it is. We may see all the negatives, but instead we need to take a fresh look and see things from a different angle.

YOUR CHALLENGE: Identify a problem that's challenged you, either with a person or an assignment. Reflect on what is not working. Now, try to see your problem from someone else's perspective. How would they solve it?

2. Too many cooks in the kitchen.

If you want to be the idea person, provide clear direction. You need implementers because they are the ones who get things done. Every idea needs to have a plan for fulfillment, a designated project lead and a timeline for completion.

YOUR CHALLENGE: At the next staff meeting, when you or someone else presents an idea, make sure there is a plan of action.

3. Keep your head on a swivel.

Always seek opportunities and possibilities for growth. Look around and head off potential problems in processes, plans, and even relationships. Opportunities are all around us!

YOUR CHALLENGE: Make today the day to identify one opportunity to improve or grow some element of your personal or professional life: find a mentor or sponsor, attend an event, read something new or develop a relationship.

BIOGRAPHY

Jeff Kubas is the Founder and President of Vertex Resource Group. Dedicated to providing exceptional, people-centered service, Jeff has established himself as a leader in the staffing industry.

Jeff and his wife Leslie founded FlexiCorps in 1992. Over 25 years, the company has experienced tremendous growth with hard work and perseverance. By embracing new opportunities, FlexiCorps was diversified by deciding to seek new types of business and through the acquisitions of other firms. Vertex Resource Group is the parent company for three staffing businesses that serve different sectors. FlexiCorps specializes in light industrial, clerical/administration, and direct recruiting for engineers, finance, and specialty tech positions. Wage Solutions offers retail staffing and payroll solutions, and Cemco is an IT and executive recruiting operation.

Every day the innovative team at Vertex provides high-caliber solutions for customers' recruiting and staffing needs across a wide variety of business sectors.

Jeff Kubas
jeffk@vertexresourcegroup.com
(630) 485-4401

SHARE ONE BEAUTIFUL, TRAGIC STORY EVERY DAY

—

Michele Kelly

"Tell your story. All of it."

The woman approached me tentatively. After all, it was a wake and wakes are hard. Strangers are compelled to comfort strangers they may never see again. Her hair matched her height; both were short. Her thick glasses magnified almond-colored eyes and took up most of her round face. I had never seen her before. A hand fell upon my arm as she said, "I knew your father. He would bring us Italian bread and sweet rolls sometimes. He always asked about my family, my kids. I'm sorry he's gone."

The "us" she was referring to was the pharmacy department

at Jewel-Osco, the local grocery store. My father's pharmacist came to his wake. On a cold, snowy, winter-ravaged night. Three days before Christmas.

I can't even get people to call me back sometimes.

For Frank Anthony LoDestro, the word "family" took on a broader meaning. My father applied the word to business, community, friends, random people who crossed his path, and, of course, my mom and my two brothers. He gave fatherly lectures to young upstarts he worked with (he was a truck driver most of his life), dropped off cans of Progresso soup to the "older" couple in the next townhome (even though they were a good ten years younger), and every Wednesday, he left a brown paper bag along the wall behind his garage. Scrawled across the bag were the words "GARBAGE MAN" in thick, black Sharpie marker; inside was a can of pop and a water bottle. He gave a bottle of Chianti and Italian bread to his accountant.

Here's what he expected in return: nothing. Here's what his life became: everything.

My father never finished eighth grade. He grew up on Chicago's South Side, in a bungalow along Moody Avenue, the youngest of nine children and the only boy. Somewhere in his life, he learned that hard work alone did not make the man. Life was about people. Showing up was not good enough or nearly as wonderful.

My father shared his beautiful, tragic story by living his values.

What do you believe in? What actions will you take to fully

express your values? If your teammates are to lead like it's their company (the acme of inspired leadership) and if building bridges with like-minded business partners is important to you and if you want to create a culture of brand believers, then trust comes by way of your choices and your choices are directed by your values. Examples: If you honor transparency, reveal your supply chain partners. If listening is a value, conduct town halls and redefine the customer experience.

My father was one of the greatest leaders I ever knew.

On the edge of his days were two sunsets — one for him and one for others.

LET YOUR BELIEFS WRITE YOUR STORY.

Fast forward to a seventy-degree day, the gray pavement solid under my feet as I ran the river trail near our home. It was Saturday and on Saturdays I run mile after mile after mile, thinking. I untie creative knots for clients and messy problems for our storytelling company. And I write. In my head. Lines of copy stream like ticker tape across my mind, words on full assault with no target save for one long stretch of blue sky.

On this particular summer day, I was thinking about our business, our "situation," as we called it.

Everything around me seemed so alive and free. The v-formation from a flock of birds overhead, flying with imperial purpose. People fishing and biking and laughing, all so content. My own legs whisked me forward without hesitation.

Inside, though, a cage of self-doubt held me captive.

Our company wasn't doing well. In short, we couldn't pay the bills. But this, in truth, was the least of our problems. We had no definition of who we were. We doubted our own value. We couldn't get clear on what we did and who we did it for. We were writers, but that seemed insignificant in a world where two million blogs are published daily. With the passage of time, I would come to understand the journey better, but not then. I saw failure and discord and hopelessness.

I was working as a freelance writer when my husband, Roderick, decided to join me as a writing and business partner in 2017. We had two skills in our back pockets: writing and reading. So we named the company K+L Storytellers. Companies are born that way sometimes. They become tangents to unlikely events. I went from being a freelance writer to CEO of a company. The regular paychecks abruptly ended. We floundered in entrepreneurial free fall with no clear idea of who we were as a company or what we were doing. Just that we needed to do something.

Through our corporate storytelling work, I have since discovered that many companies struggle with a lack of clarity.

Simon Sinek made finding your "why" relevant, but it is rarely phrased that way. The words are much more poignant. People say, *"I don't know if I'm doing the right things. What if I'm just wasting all my time? How am I making a difference with what I do every day? Am I headed in the right direction?"*

Purpose taps us on the shoulder in the quiet of night or those early morning musings, before our day jettisons us forward, and asks, what gives? We wonder, doubt, and challenge ourselves. Mostly, we just wonder.

As I ran that day, a tiny idea spread over me like the heat from the sun warming the back of my neck. That tiny idea came from a thousand tiny voices from conversations spanning a lifetime.

It was my mother's voice telling me she loved the songs I wrote on my guitar. It was my father's voice telling me about the strength of my Italian immigrant grandparents. It was the voice of my brothers who said I could be anything just by dreaming it. It was the final goodnight from my three everythings who fell asleep to my made-up bedtime stories.

And then I listened to my own voice and this is what it said: *You give hope by finding the beauty in people's stories.* This had always been my purpose. Suddenly, leading K+L Storytellers became exciting, no longer a burden.

I discovered, quite by accident, that our purpose is defined by how we impact others and the story we share every day in our work. This is not brilliant or ground-breaking. It's remarkably simple, and I'm sure a multitude of people before me have come to the same conclusion.

One would think I should have already figured this out. But I think that's how it goes for most of us. A thousand people could say something magnificent, but when we discover it ourselves it feels like we're Einstein the moment he discovered relativity.

You know how you've really found your "why," though? You cry. And that's exactly what I did. I ran and I cried, and the tears burned my cheeks. I was the lucky girl to find the story of others.

I remember the exact spot on the trail that day, the direction of the wind, and the vividness of the green grass and purple yellow flowers along the river. I smelled the gritty earth and the river's watery dampness.

When I returned home, I knew we would be OK. No one could have given me that answer. My "why" was inside me all along.

And yours is inside you, too.

MAKE YOUR "WHY" THE HEART OF YOUR STORY.

As a ghostwriter, I assume the persona of others in books and blogs, emails, and newsletters. I am a ghost. Whoooosh go the words, and they are no longer mine.

I have noticed among some C-suite executives this fear of being honest. Many want to tell the truth, but only enough to get by. I beg you: Tell your story. All of it. Don't leave out the messy parts, the times you struggled, your downfalls, the moments you wanted to give up, the failures. These are life's natural reminders we are not infallible.

These are the moments that make our companies human.

A few years ago, I blogged for a tech company. Its content was very customer-focused; its voice very human. Then came the interview that put the kibosh on everything, as my Italian grandmother would say.

I happened to interview the CEO at a point when,

unbeknownst to me, there were changes afoot. I ghostwrote a blog for Patrick about how they had cut prices to keep customers through the recession. They had actually met with every single one to discuss what they could do to help them. In the blog post, I mentioned the fear and anxiety Patrick had felt, all of which was true.

When I got the piece back, he had struck each line revealing the truth. What remained were words anyone could have written. And that's the big secret. Our brokenness makes our story beautiful. I could not convince the CEO of this.

Less than a year later, an SEO-driven marketing agency took over and loaded the tech company's blogs with keywords. This oftentimes is like putting lipstick on an orangutan. Headlines are stiff. Copy is plastic. Keyword overload is like an annoying skip on a scratched album.

The move was uncharacteristic of the company I once knew and was one of many culture-shifting decisions which, I believe, stemmed from an urgent desire to look like everybody else.

Hide failures. Bury vulnerability. Ignore humanity.

I call it the "egg" complex. Open a carton of eggs, and what do you see? Sameness. Carton after carton, it's a sea of white.

Here is the rest of the story about that tech firm.

The content no longer served his clients but bowed to the SEO gods. The company went from being story-driven to sales-driven, an outward-facing steward to an inward-facing brand. The homepage became self-congratulatory.

What happens when you take all your inadequacies and

tuck them away? You look like everybody else in business. White shell, smooth finish, oval-shaped.

In contrast, the second book I ghostwrote was for a man who had the courage to share his humanity. He told me within the first hour of our meeting that he wanted to save people from making the mistakes he had made.

So he shared. He spoke about leaving his wife, not being there for his daughter, putting winning above all else, and drinking too much. His book garnered nearly one hundred comments from people who felt changed by his words. Would he have accomplished this by hiding his pains and failures? You know the answer.

When you give a part of yourself with words, you are courageously trusting the reader.

Trust matters to most companies. The word sits like a pompous guest at dinner in vision statements and website headlines, but are these the right seats? Shouldn't trust sit at the head of the table as a humble host?

If you want to be trusted, trust. Trust that people won't dismiss you for being human. Treat trust as a coveted emotion to be earned rather than a purchase to be made. Inspire trust in your actions and words every day. Tell your story.

We cannot be takers. We must be givers.

This applies to business colleagues, customers, influencers, and workmates. It applies to our mates, our children, friends, and our community.

Brave does not mean fearless. Brave means the company

you lead has the unrivaled determination and courage to be true to its core, flaws included.

YOUR FAULT LINES MAKE YOUR STORY BEAUTIFUL.

We are all broken. Don't be ashamed.

It is mostly universal that we all want to make a difference. As a corporate storyteller, we call this the philosophical problem for a company.

Katherine didn't know about philosophy. The seventh grader just knew her father had taken his own life the year before. We will come back to Katherine in a moment because she, more than anyone else in my career, has taught me the tenet of being an inspired leader. Katherine taught me that philosophical problems in business are as important as a company's valuation, revenue projections, and bottom line.

Back to philosophy. The Canadian Broadcasting Corporation produced a radio episode entitled, "Why Businesses Are Hiring Philosophers to Help Their Bottom Line." It turns out that philosophers are helping CEOs make strategic decisions because they create meaning with a broader set of worldly ideas.

Forward-thinking companies all around us address philosophical problems. Tesla hits on sustainability. Starbucks builds community. Patagonia protects our earth. Philosophical problems are big problems no one person — or one company — can solve. But one can try — even just a little. You can move the pieces forward in how you operate, build culture, hire people, choose supply chain partners, produce a product or service.

What philosophical problems matter to you as a leader? What legacy do you wish to leave?

For me, the philosophical problem has been a generation of youth who are not encouraged to write more than 140 characters. They've been duped by technology stealing their time to dream. English teachers (if you are one, please don't take offense, I am merely pointing out a flaw in an archaic educational system) whose thick, red markers bleed young writers' chances of being creatively confident; and an obsession in our culture to measure success by points on a scoreboard (GPA, ACT, SAT, class rank) rather than imagination.

Where do we honor the visionaries, thinkers, dreamers, writers, artists, creators?

This is how I came to meet Katherine (I've changed a few details out of respect for the writer) through a young author's program I created in 2016 called Your Extraordinary Story or YES for short. Katherine's story is a tragic one, but it doesn't have to end that way. She can write a new ending to her story. And she did.

In YES, I teach short story writing workshops for middle school students. Now, you might be shocked to hear that I've never published a short story, and I don't have a master's of fine arts from Northwestern University or University of Iowa. I've never published a fiction book in my life (it is on my bucket list though).

There's just this: a deep desire to share one beautiful, tragic story every day. I do this by inspiring others to do the same.

Leadership does not begin the day you take the title. It begins when you are a child. Who was he, this child-self? How did time vanish? What did you love to create?

When I was seven, I wrote a book entitled *Watch Out World, Here Comes My Thoughts* (the term "book" is being generous; it was a sheaf of typed papers connected by a rusty staple). I went on to write short stories about a beautiful girl named Eleanor (no idea why I was obsessed with this name). I wrote songs on my guitar about unrequited love in high school (including one titled *You Gotta Kiss A Lot of Frogs Before You Meet Prince Charming*, which I'm sure would have climbed the charts had anyone but my mother heard it).

I was an overweight, introverted loner in my youth who hid behind books and words. Words, in many ways, saved me.

As in the time a boy asked me to dance at an eighth-grade party (I was shocked I was even invited) and, upon my surprised "yes," then walked away with a smirk on his face (right, I'm still a bit salty about this).

All this to say that developing a young author's program was born from my own battle scars and love of words. The YES program is less about writing a great story and more about rewriting life's possibilities. This came to light in Katherine's story.

When the authors and I talked about her story's ending, some suggested her main character (a serial killer named Peter) might end up not wanting to murder anymore. She paused and said, "Why is it there's never a story about a bad guy winning for who he is?"

Katherine wants the bad guy to win. She's making sense of her father's actions and rewriting life's possibilities.

In business, it's called corporate social responsibility. I call it being human, living your purpose, and sharing your beautiful, tragic story.

Find the people who need your talents. Then do something. This is what Katherine taught me. Bring your talents to the underserved, the ones who least expect you to show up.

Be a flash mob. Like a choir bursting into song at a mall. Make a scene.

If you are an operational genius, help a food pantry optimize workflow. If you are an inspiring speaker, teach college students to be communicative wunderkinds. If you are a technology aficionado—organize a tele-summit to mentor tech entrepreneurs.

You've been there. Your passion is in your work. Take your talents to the people.

Not to scale in twelve months. Not to be famous. Not to make a pile of money. But because it's our one chance to leave the world better than we found it.

Your story is your one, true legacy as a leader.

TURN YOUR TALENTS INTO GOOD
ON A MASSIVE SCALE.

Your company story wasn't dropped from the sky. It came by way of hard work and falling down, successes and failures, right decisions and short-sighted mistakes, and all-night panic sessions.

Your story is beautiful and tragic and enduring. No one else has your story. It's the only one in the whole world and you are the only one who has the honor of telling it. Your legacy as a leader hinges not on revenues and valuation, but how you leave the world when you walk away from it. This is your story well-lived.

MENTORSHIP MOMENT

"Your story is beautiful and tragic and enduring. No one else has your story. It's the only one in the whole world and you are the only one who has the honor of telling it. Your legacy as a leader hinges, not on revenues and valuation, but how you leave the world when you walk away from it. This is your story well-lived."

REFLECTION: Explore your beautiful, tragic story and the value of sharing it with others.

- What values are important to you as a leader?
- How do these values influence your actions and decisions?
- Does your team "see" your values through your actions?

- Do you share stories of struggle, hope, your youth, failure, triumph with your team?
- Do you encourage story sharing in your company?
- Why do you lead? Once you've answered this question, ask "why" at least three more times.
- Do you hide behind what others expect you to be?
- Do you feel like it's more important to be right than to be honest?
- How are your using your talents to do good for others in unexpected ways?
- How are you inspiring others inside and outside your organization to share their story?

BIOGRAPHY

Michele Kelly, (a.k.a "The Word Girl") got her start as a freelance writer interviewing Chicago Bears players for *Playgirl Magazine*. Being the youngest and only girl in an Italian family, she paper-clipped the pages to show her parents the article and was almost never let out of the house again. Today, Michele is co-founder and CEO of K+L Storytellers, a company passionate about brand story and kick-A content for middle market companies hungry to scale.

Michele has ghostwritten three books and cranks out more than 10,000 words of copy for companies each month with the same urgency as Wonder Woman saving the world with words. She is a contributing writer to the online magazine *SalesPOP!*, authors a blog called "Sunday Pasta" about life and business, and has just enough unfinished manuscripts lying around to label her an aspiring novelist.

In 2016, she launched Your Extraordinary Story, a young

authors program that has inspired more than 100 young people to write short stories. While she gives more than 50 speeches a year on story, her favorite stage is lecturing their three children and sharing story love with husband and business partner, Roderick Kelly.

Michele Kelly
michele@klstorytellers.com
(630) 697-2562
Twitter: @mkellywriter

LEADING THROUGH LIFE'S CURVES

—

Jim "O" Oberhofer

"Good leaders help others become the best they can be."

"Hey, Jim, this guy wants to talk to you."

It was my brother Jon, motioning to a man standing just beyond the ropes that separated the racing fans from those of us in the pit at the National Hot Rod Association (NHRA) Gatornationals in Gainesville, Florida. I was there with Kalitta Motorsports as the crew chief for Doug Kalitta's Mac Tools Top Fuel dragster. I walked over to the stranger, a man about 15 years older than myself who looked clearly shaken or nervous, I couldn't tell which. He introduced himself, and with eyes filled with sorrow, said, "I've recently lost my wife of more than 40 years to cancer." I immediately felt his struggle and knew why he had sought me out. I had lost my beautiful wife Tammy, just a few years earlier, to the same monster.

He was obviously struggling and seeking direction. I remembered that horrible feeling. Mentally pushing aside my pre-race "to do" list, I ushered him past the ropes and into the hospitality area reserved for VIPs. There he poured out his heart to me and I offered the words of encouragement I could. I told him it would get better. Grieving is good and so is crying. For me, talking about Tammy was great medicine. Would talking about his wife help? Most of all, I told him to reach out for support. Afterwards, his eyes looked a little brighter. And I told him to keep in touch, which he did.

He wasn't the only one who ever approached me to share their story. I wrote my book, *Top Fuel For Life: Life Lessons From a Crew Chief*, to help other people deal with their loss and mistakes, but I never expected to reach so many. I've received emails, letters, and phone calls from grieving husbands, wives, parents, siblings, all thanking me for sharing my story. People have approached me at races to get their book autographed, but also shared their struggle with loss. I remember being a little nervous about writing the book, but I decided if it helped just one person, it would all be worth it. Mission accomplished.

Top Fuel tells stories of my triumphs, failures, joys, and tears during more than three decades of working in the racing world. I write about meeting Tammy, and the birth of our daughter, Ashley. I write about starting my career at age sixteen as a parts washer, and eventually becoming crew chief and VP of Operations at Kalitta. I also write about how my obsession with winning took over my life, costing me my family and my happiness. And I write about how it all helped me become a better leader and focus on what matters most. I learned the hard way that good leaders help others become the best they can be.

DEPARTURES AND ARRIVALS

In September of 2018, after more than three decades on their team, I parted ways with Kalitta Motorsports. It's scary to leave your comfort zone, but it was time. My initial plan was to take a break from racing, then go into business for myself, but I was open to suggestions!

After the news broke of my split with Kalitta Motorsports, the phone started ringing. One of the first calls was from my friend Jim Harrington of Victory Lane Quick Oil Change Centers out of Plymouth, Michigan. Jim is the VP of New Franchising, and he told me they were looking to expand into the Dallas/Fort Worth, Texas area, near my hometown of Plano. He asked me if I was interested in becoming a new franchisee. I absolutely was!

A move back to Texas felt like the right thing to do. Early in 2018, my dad, who raised both my brother and I in the drag racing world and was our inspiration, had to undergo major back surgery. Because of my racing schedule, I was unable to be there for him or help my mom while he was recovering. This happened all too often during my racing career, and it really bothered me this time. Starting a business in Texas would also allow me to spend more time with my baby sister Susie O, who lived nearby in Fort Worth. She was especially excited about my potential move back home and couldn't wait to spend more time with her big brother. My daughter, Ashley, was on her own, living in Indianapolis, and gave the move her blessing. But no sooner was I sure of my decision when my fun-loving, free spirited sister unexpectedly passed away on February 12, 2019. Susie was such a force of nature with a voice that rivaled some of the great female vocalists in the music industry. Her death at only forty-nine years old was devastating to us all, and a sign that life is too short to take for granted.

Then I received another call, this time from my good friend Paul Lee, a veteran Funny Car driver I first met while working at Kalitta. Paul is amazing. Here was a guy who lived through a heart attack that people in the medical profession refer to as "the widow maker." He thought he would never drive again. But with the right medical care and Paul's never-say-die attitude, he was given a clean bill of health. Now he wanted to start his own Funny Car team and he wanted me to be the crew chief. How could I accept? I would have to be in Texas for my business.

Then out of the blue, I received a call from Doug Stringer, the owner of Clay Millican's Top Fuel Dragster team. He asked me if I would be interested in joining them as a consultant for the new crew chief on Clay's car for the 2019 season, and then eventually becoming the crew chief of a new Funny Car team with one of their marketing partners. The marketing partner turned out to be Paul Lee! Everything was lining up so nicely, but I told him my obstacle, which was moving to Texas for my business. Doug said, "Hey, you wouldn't have to be here; you could just fly in and out for the races." So I could work with my buddy Paul Lee and help Doug get Clay's car back on track? Yes, please!

I had always been curious about working on Funny Cars, which vary greatly from Top Fuel dragsters. Both are the fastest accelerating, piston-driven machines on earth, with eleven-thousand horsepower, fueled with nitromethane and able to reach speeds of three hundred and thirty miles per hour miles per hour while covering one thousand feet in under four seconds. The motor sits in front of the driver of a Funny Car, with a shorter, one hundred and twenty-five-inch wheelbase chassis and a carbon fiber shell atop the chassis to replicate a typical car. By comparison, the Top Fuel dragsters have a three-hundred-inch wheelbase chassis with carbon fiber body panels and a giant, rear wing providing downforce, with the motor sitting behind the driver. Top Fuel dragsters require a more aggressive tuning approach and a driver with a lot of talented precision and finesse. Funny cars require a more finessed tuning approach and a driver who is aggressive enough to keep all that power under control. In my opinion, both are the coolest racecars on the planet!

I imagined holidays with my brother, Jon, the Co-Crew Chief of two Championship Funny Car Teams at Kalitta. Would he remain the most successful Funny Car crew chief in the family? I had to find out, so I accepted the offer!

LEADERS AND COMMANDERS

As I prepared for my first day as the new crew chief for

Paul's Funny Car, I flashed back to that day at Kalitta when a younger version of myself met the new crew chief of Scott Kalitta's Top Fuel dragster. Dick LaHaie was a slight, sandy-haired thinker who knew his way around Top Fuel dragsters and people too. Poor Dick certainly had his work cut out for himself. First, he hadn't hired any of us; he had inherited us. He didn't know our skill set or what we could do. Yet his mission was to take a bunch of misfits and teach us how to be champions.

In the drag racing world, the crew chief is typically older than the crew members, which creates some interesting dynamics. Crew chiefs typically rise up through the ranks, just as I had. I joined Kalitta when I was only twenty-one years old, and I did my time cleaning parts, building short blocks, assembling cylinder heads, and laying the groundwork for new crew members. My experience commanded respect because I understood what the new guys were going through. But in the corporate world, it's not always like that.

People meet their new leader and they think, where did he/she come from? How did they get put in charge of me? What have they done? But whether or not your qualifications to lead are obvious or not, it's important to earn the respect of your subordinates before you can expect them to follow.

Dick did this by showing respect for each of our contributions. He taught us how important every little job or piece was on a Top Fuel car. I also learned a really important lesson from him: don't focus on what people can't do; find out what they are good at and let them do it!

I truly believe there is good in everybody; you just have to find it. For example, you might hire a new crew member to do cylinder heads on the race car, but even after being taught, he stills struggles. Instead of giving up on him, take the time to find out his strength. For example, he may do a great job building shortblocks. Then you understand where to position him to excel on the team.

In my early days, people took time to teach and mentor me, even when things didn't come naturally. They understood that my mistakes were all part of my learning process before I could move forward. The important thing is to mentor each other to become the best we can be, especially when we are in a leadership position. When you allow people to succeed, their confidence grows, and they can contribute their full potential.

It's all part of treating people the way you would want to be treated. You have to respect people at the place they are in their life, whether they are a CEO or an intern. By showing respect, you earn respect. And respect is the fuel for great leadership. Those who rule without respect, are what I call "commanders."

Commanders lead by intimidation, dishonesty, and belittling their subordinates. They won't admit wrong in any situation. Instead, they fabricate a story to keep themselves in the right. True leaders, who have the respect of their subordinates, can admit they are wrong and still save face. That's because their employees will continue to respect them and remember their integrity, not their failing.

Commanders also ask things of their subordinates that they

would not do themselves. People will be most likely to perform a task if they believe you think it's valuable to the mission. This could be anything from scrubbing a toilet to handling a complaint face-to-face. Here's where leading by example comes in. Commanders say, "do it." But leaders will actually go do it themselves if they must. And, they will show appreciation to those who act in their place.

One of the hardest roles of a leader is to be a mediator, having to decide who is right about a certain issue. As my leadership responsibility at Kalitta grew from supervising ten employees to eighty, my need to mediate did too. Dissension in the ranks is destructive to any team, and it's the leader who must bring it to an end.

The leader has the last word, right? When there's an argument, you must listen to two, three, or four sides of a story, and eventually make a decision. Your enemy in this scenario is the knee jerk reaction (KJR). You know what I'm talking about? It's that desire to react immediately, with a decision, panic, emotional collapse or a few loud, choice four-letter words. Leaders have to avoid the KJR at all costs.

Instead, know there are multiple sides to any issue. If you let one side influence your thinking prematurely, it will lead to a KJR or wrong decision that can weaken your team. Instead, when people come to you with a problem, remember that it is the most important thing in the world to them at the moment. I keep this in mind and listen very carefully, trying to figure out who the problem is truly affecting. Just the employee? The entire team?

The company? Then I do my best to consider all sides of the argument, gathering as much information as I can and bringing in other people for opinions.

Finally, when I feel I have all the facts, I consider the problem from all angles and make a final judgement. My decision won't please everyone and I accept that. All leaders must. You can't be everyone's pal and they won't always be happy with your decisions. So I communicate my decision with care and respect. If I do that well, those who disagree with me will at least feel heard.

NEW CHALLENGES, NEW IMPACT

One of the things I loved about working for Kalitta was the ability to make an impact on people. I'm not necessarily talking about winning a race. I'm talking about making somebody's day. Like giving a kid a close-up view of the pit crew in action and putting a smile on their face. Or giving an executive a backstage tour of the magic and delighting in their wide-eyes and arched eyebrows when we reveal how it all happens. I look forward to these same things with my three new leadership projects: consulting with Clay Millican, being crew chief for Paul Lee, and opening the oil change franchises. I'm stepping out of the comfort zone of Kalitta, but I'm ready. I'm bringing everything I know and love about racing and leadership to tackle all the challenges that come my way.

As a consultant for Clay Millican's Top Fuel car, I'm there to help and add value where I can, based on my vast experience. When I first arrived, I wondered, *what did I get myself into?* With significant turnover in the crew, the operation was in complete disarray. But I have a pair of strong, rose-colored glasses which I got from working at Kalitta. I've always been a positive person and I needed to truly understand the team before they could see what I saw in them. So I took time to get to know the crew, what makes them tick, and what my role should be. It's been a challenge and a lot of fun to see them now pull for the same goal with focus and a positive attitude.

And you know what? It's working!

In our first round race at the Arizona Nationals, we smoked the tires but learned some important things about the car. At our next race in Gainesville, Florida, we made it to the final round of the Gatornationals, then did it again a few weeks later at the Four-Wide Nationals in Las Vegas.

But in racing, you're only as good as your last run. It's going to be a long, grueling season and we are up against lots of great cars, teams, and drivers. My main goal is to make sure I'm a positive influence for the team. Win or lose, I want to make sure our team is happy with the race and prepared to keep doing even better. That's what winning is really all about.

I'm realistic. Both Clay and Paul's teams are a far cry from the big time programs with solid financial backing and a depth of parts that we are competing against. What we lack, we make up for in passion and determination. It's the crew chief's challenge to make magic, no matter what they have to work with. We know winning an NHRA race would be like the worst team in the NFL winning against the Patriots.

On Paul's team, our secret weapon is our passion to make Paul a winner. It's surreal to be crew chief in a brand new organization, but Paul's faith and confidence in me has given me the motivation needed for this team to succeed! He's been given a new lease on life and we can't wait till the car is ready and we can take our place on the track and make every race count for him!

As for challenge number three, the oil change shops, I'm looking forward to diving into that unchartered territory too. My goal is to open three locations in Dallas within the next five years, and apply all of the leadership lessons I've learned in drag racing to operate the best franchise around with my own winning team.

I've come a long way to become the leader I am today. But if I live each day trying to make someone's life a little better, I know I'm being the best leader I can be.

MENTORSHIP MOMENT

Wouldn't it be great to always lead like a champion?

I'll be honest. I've seen a lot of champions. And I've seen a lot of asses. What's the difference? Here's my take on it. If you agree, take it to heart and start living this way. If not, email me and we'll talk.

Being a champion isn't all about winning. Victory is fleeting, but figuring out how to win next time after you've lost is what true champions do.

Being a champion means showing up as a leader at home and at work. If you put happiness first, you will get this in the right order, with the right balance.

Being a champion means showing you have faith in your team. That means showing, not just telling. It means standing up for them and supporting them when they need it.

Being a champion means staying the course with a positive attitude. If you think you're going to lose the next race, guess what? You probably will. Stay positive.

Being a champion means sharing your passion. I hope that by sharing, I can help others steer clear of the mistakes I have made. It's the reason I wrote *Top Fuel for Life* and the reason I'm in this book.

It's not easy to lead like a champion. But I found it was a lot harder and more painful not to do so.

BIOGRAPHY

Jim Oberhofer, known throughout the racing world as "Jim O," is one of the most sought after crew chiefs on the NHRA circuit with more than 80 race wins and three championships as a crew-member, crew chief, and general manager.

Jim O currently consults on the NHRA circuit with Clay Millican's Parts Plus Top Fuel dragster and serves as crew chief on Paul Lee's McLeod Funny Car.

Oberhofer recently published *Top Fuel for Life: Life Lessons from a Crew Chief,* a memoir about life, love and the loss of his wife, Tammy, to cancer. He established the Tammy O Foundation, which sends funds to organizations close to Tammy O's heart, including B.R.AK.E.S., Pandas International, Racers For Christ, DRAW, and the Infinite Hero Foundation.

Jim enjoys ballroom dancing and loves to spend time with his grown daughter, Ashley. He is looking forward to opening franchise locations of Victory Lane Quick Change shops in the Dallas area.

Jim Oberhofer
Jimoberhofer.com
(734) 657-8850

TRAILBLAZING FOR GOOD

Neli Vazquez Rowland

"The genuine show of leadership is action."

I walk into the lobby of A Safe Haven and I'm greeted by Nicole. She's volunteering today at the concierge desk, greeting guests and people in crisis who come to A Safe Haven seeking help. Today, she is beautiful, kind, poised, and smart. But not long ago, she herself shuffled through the doors of A Safe Haven looking beaten and scared, addicted to drugs and alcohol, with her life hanging by a thread.

For over 15 years, her parents had tried everything to help Nicole break her addictions, from tough love to "club med" type treatment programs. Yet after rehab she would return to their loving care and affluent, Connecticut suburb only to relapse again. And again. With battered, broken hearts, they looked on helplessly, on edge every time the phone rang and Nicole wasn't home, thinking it was the hospital...or worse. Out of desperation and in fear for Nicole's life, they searched nationally for something different, something that could reach her, and they found it with A Safe Haven (ASH) in Chicago. "My parents found me living on the streets and I didn't want to go," recalls Nicole, "but they told me I was either going to go there, or to the cemetery. It saved my life."

Today, Nicole is successfully receiving treatment and working on her recovery. She's working towards self-sufficiency and looking forward to reuniting with her 14-year-old daughter. "I have never seen a place anything like this in the country. There needs to be one in every city," said Nicole. Her story is poignant, and one of more than 120,000 stories from people we have met and whose lives have been transformed since my husband Brian and I opened ASH 25 years ago!

We never set out to be advocates for the homeless population, yet as founders of ASH, that is what we have become. We continue our original mission and social enterprise model that helps people aspire, transform and sustain their lives as they transition from homelessness to self-sufficiency with pride and purpose.

Today, ASH is lauded as truly the most vertically integrated and comprehensive social service, social enterprise and phased-housing model in the country. We help lift people into self-sufficiency by providing the opportunity and resources to address and overcome their root causes of poverty and homelessness through a holistic and scalable model. ASH's visible social and economic impact restores lives, unites families, stabilizes neighborhoods, and creates vibrant, viable communities.

Central to the development of ASH is the belief in running our own race after becoming a subject matter expert, and integrating leadership, vision and a pioneering spirit into all our efforts.

RUN YOUR OWN RACE

I learned to run my own race at my first job. I was a newly trained, green-around-the-gills stock broker, cold calling for commissions at an investment firm with a highly competitive, cutthroat culture. It was the late 1980's and through a stroke of luck, I had been able to attend college and become the first in my family of seven immigrant children to graduate. My friend Mike worked at the investment firm too, and Brian (who was just a friend back then) had arranged the interview for me and believed that I would succeed, even before I did. There I was, with no other role model than my parents who taught me to work hard, be honest, help others and believe in God.

The attrition rate at the firm was high and a physical leaderboard on the wall told everyone exactly how successful you were. Weeks turned into months and I stayed right at the bottom. In a last-ditch effort to save me, my manager moved me next to Lexi, a woman slightly my senior who was succeeding.

At first, she ignored me, but I didn't take it personally since the attrition rate was so high, you weren't deemed worth talking to until you proved you could do the job. (Today, she is still one of my best friends!) I kept my ear cocked to Lexi's conversations, trying to glean whatever secrets she could give me for closing a sale. But then one day I had an epiphany. I realized that if I was going to succeed, I didn't need to look around or eavesdrop more; I needed to don some blinders and find my own style. I wasn't doing well anyway, so what did I have to lose?

I knew I was different from everyone else at the firm. I was one of a few women and the only Latina there. Many of my co-workers had come from affluent families and college-bound neighborhoods. Some of them had parents who had pulled strings to get them started. I was first-generation from Mexican immigrants. My neighborhood was beset with gangs, addicts, and crime and college wasn't even originally in my plans.

I decided my only chance was to run my own race. I was going to take an inventory of what I knew made me different, and then use it to my advantage. The fun part about being the underdog is nobody was waiting for me to succeed. So when I finally did, I completely blindsided them. They never saw me coming!

Real success started with a trip to Mexico to visit my mother. I opened the newspaper to read about an upcoming election with a candidate named Salinas, a Harvard graduate who was interested in privatizing the telephone company and other government-owned infrastructure companies in Mexico. I had already noticed that many of my mother's neighbors would come over to use her phone throughout the day because it was too expensive to have one in their own home. In fact, only one in 20 homes actually had a phone....in the twentieth century! Suddenly I saw that this Harvard graduate candidate might open an opportunity for investors to make money if the election went his way. My natural curiosity would not rest.

To my mother's complete surprise, I hopped a 12-hour hour bus ride from her hometown in the State of Jalisco and traveled to "La Bolsa," the home of the Mexican stock exchange in Mexico City. I introduced myself as vice president of a large investment firm from America and proceeded to gather information on the financial projections of the telephone company, "Telefonos de Mexico" TELMEX. I convinced my Mexican colleagues to fax me the information daily about their markets in Spanish, which I could read.

Confident that my research was sound, I seized the opportunity, began investing in anticipation of the election and rejoiced when my candidate won and my investments started to produce results. But my managers were less than pleased with these "emerging markets." They felt that the corruption, political and financial climate of Mexico posed a high risk for investors, even though my stocks were trading at 1/10 th of book value and low-price earnings ratios relative to the growth potential. Indeed, my portfolio was a much safer bet than many of the investments the firm touted! They even had me make my investors sign a waiver, releasing the firm from responsibility for losses, with a promise from me that I would be solely liable. I was undeterred, because I was confident and seeing the future.

Guess what happened next? My stocks continued to double and triple in value, and I took my place as the firm's Mexican emerging market specialist. I flew up the leaderboards and differentiated myself in this area, all from deciding to run my own race instead of doing things the same as everyone else.

Real redemption came when NAFTA passed in the early 90's and my Mexican stocks were now trading on the New York Stock Exchange and being recommended by my firm.

BECOME A SUBJECT MATTER EXPERT

My 13 years of training in the financial world taught me to find supporting research for my ideas to help me make decisions, and to keep my ears and eyes open for data and trends to lead me to bigger and better things.

In the early 90's, I was the mother of a four-year-old boy and pregnant with my second son. My husband Brian and I were financially comfortable, and being young parents, we wanted to do something to give back to the community and also take advantage of the buyers' market in real estate. We decided to purchase a distressed, thirteen-unit building near the Logan Square area of Chicago, rehab it and allow people suffering from substance abuse addiction to live there for free. Why house people with substance abuse issues? Because the problem was near and dear to us.

Brian was an army veteran who had struggled with alcoholism in his college years and had been fortunate to be able to get into an exclusive treatment program, covered by his medical insurance. I also knew, because of my humble upbringing, that too many lives were lost to the disease when it went untreated. So our vision and mission to help people suffering with addiction became personal.

From firsthand experience, we also knew that treatment programs were expensive. Our hearts went out to those who had neither the resources nor the professional support in an environment conducive to recovery to break their addiction. Instead, they quickly slipped into the marginalized populations of our society.

We took the personal risk and invested our own money in multiple apartment complexes in distressed communities, when banks would not lend us money to build housing for recovering addicts. We rehabbed the apartment buildings, furnished them nicely, and even professionally landscaped the property throughout so our residents would have the dignified accommodations we envisioned for them. Our plan was to eventually sell the buildings when the market turned, but we soon saw how important the residence was to those living there, and it felt heartless to walk away. Besides, there is never a good time to stop helping people. So that's how A Safe Haven was born!

The biggest eye-opener for us was the people we attracted. We expected people from the inner city, products of a long family history of addiction. Instead, we found people who had led seemingly normal lives before becoming homeless. They were suburban housewives with children, who once had a stable relationship and a home but through an accident, were prescribed addictive pain relievers that took over their lives. They were veterans, who had served their country, fought bravely, and returned home only to face the overwhelming challenges of finding employment, housing, and addiction to opioids or alcohol. There were young people, full of potential, who lost an affluent life because of a bad decision that led to a habit and alienated their entire support system. Hopelessly addicted and "dope sick," many of our residents had broken the law to support their habit and now had a prison record that kept them finding employment. We were witnessing the birth of the opioid epidemic, decades before it was ever declared a national emergency.

Our research surrounding the War on Drugs found there were few plans to treat addiction; just to deal with the consequences. The government strengthened laws against drug-related crimes and began increasing prison capacity in anticipation of a new generation of criminals based on the third-grade reading levels of children in the public schools. The system was broken. Like standing in the tracks of an oncoming train, we saw how the growth of an addicted population would derail not only the lives of people, but the financial well-being of all areas of society, including healthcare, educational and criminal justice systems, gang activity, housing, and unemployment. Today, the American prison population makes up 24 percent of the world prison population (ranking us at #1), even though the U.S. makes up only five percent of the world's population.

Early on, we learned that providing shelter was not enough. How can anyone move to self-sufficiency if their underlying problem, the addiction, is not addressed? Any one unable to find affordable treatment can lose their job and end up homeless on the street, breaking the law to support their habit. How could they ever recover and break out of the system, without treatment? Without treating the underlying behavioral health issues of substance abuse, which may include the spectrum of depression, mental health, and trauma, an addict can never take the other steps to self-sufficiency and improve his/her life through education and job training, finding gainful employment, and stable housing.

When we looked around to donate to a sustainable model to address and solve these issues holistically, we found none. Could we create our own? Our answer was yes.

We began by hiring Skip, a highly-trained professional to treat our homeless residents, and it was overwhelmingly successful. We decided the State needed standards of care, so we helped create licensure for our field and then became the State's first licensed recovery home. We listened and filled in the gaps of our residents' lives, connecting the dots to their self-sufficiency. When we needed funding beyond what the government could provide, private donors and investors stepped in.

Once our residents were successfully in recovery, we needed compassionate employers willing to take a chance on our residents who often had police records. We wondered, who would hire these people? Then we realized, we could!

We began investing in social enterprises, a business that makes a profit but also provides an added social benefit. We acquired and began growing a landscaping company which offered gainful, meaningful employment to help residents bridge to self-sufficiency. Today, our ASH-operated organizations also include a landscaping business, a catering business and a staffing service company. Our socially responsible corporate customer and employer partner organizations are proud to be doing something strategically significant to help solve the problem of homelessness by simply hiring our residents or contracting with our social enterprises.

The final piece of our self-sufficiency puzzle was to provide a phased, real estate development model which now allows people to move seamlessly from transitional, supportive, affordable, senior and veteran housing, based on their unique circumstances.

ASH is a smart investment for the public, because we save taxpayer money by moving a resident through our system to self-sufficiency for much less than taxpayers pay to keep someone cycling in and out of homelessness, emergency rooms, hospitals or the criminal justice system. Also, through ASH, most of our residents complete our program in months and move on to gainful employment and permanent housing much sooner and more seamlessly than the incarcerated individuals who remain in prison for years.

MAKING OF A TRAILBLAZER

In the business world today, we tend to use the words "visionary," "leader," "pioneer," and "trailblazer" interchangeably, don't we? But to me, the genuine show of leadership is action. A visionary is the person who thinks, "Wouldn't it be great if we could go to the moon?" But it's the leader who says, "This is how we're going to get to the moon," puts a team together and builds the rocket. The pioneer is the first one on board to take the trip. I think to be a true trailblazer, you need to be all three—a visionary who is a leader through action with a pioneering spirit.

Brian and I were visionaries when we conceived of the

model for ASH, a unique, vertically integrated service model to lift the homeless to self-sufficiency with all the services they need under one roof. We were leaders by investing our own dollars into the project, which helped gain additional investors, staff, supporters, and partners who helped us house, feed, treat, educate, train, employ, encourage, support, and empower our residents. Our college friend, Mark, joined us as partner and COO and others joined as part of our leadership, board of directors, or advisory board. Many more are helping us amplify our mission to make a significant social impact. Momentum is finally building and accelerating our cause. Finally, we pioneered (and our still pioneering!) our program by necessity because there was no other model.

We are still running our own race and have served more than 120,000 people, averaging about 5,000 residents a year, since our opening. We average almost 1,000 job placements a year through our staffing social enterprise and our residents are regularly referred by our funders including jail, prison, human service agencies, the Veterans Administration and former residents, and hospital social workers, who see people with the potential to live independently with the help of treatment and support. Due to capacity restrictions and funding constraints, we are unfortunately always full and on average we turn away 1,000 adults, single moms with children, non-violent re-entry individuals, veterans, and others, every month. This is unacceptable to us.

We are at a pivotal moment in our nation's history.

Government responds to public pressure so it will take a groundswell of support from the public to ensure society prioritizes the issues of the opioid and homeless epidemics and the need for more affordable housing. We must stay committed to these urgent causes and allocate resources towards proven best practices (like ASH) to move the needle in the right direction.

In our 25 years, we have beaten the drum to change the conversation and the national dialogue around the issues we address and we are happy that our model is no longer going unnoticed. We have won a collection of awards for our social and economic innovation, community impact, and humanitarianism. For example, we are proud to have been recognized as a "Champion of Change" by the White House under President Obama in 2013. I was honored to be nominated for the award by Rotary International, and in 2019, I was also honored with an invitation to speak at the White House Opportunity Zone Conference, along with Cabinet members, to address a bipartisan audience of state and local leaders, mayors, county commissioners, economic development officers, entrepreneurs, faith leaders, and tribal leaders. After being introduced by President Trump, I began my speech by saying, "A Safe Haven was founded with this day in mind." I shared our success story, creating jobs and affordable housing in opportunity zones where ASH primarily invests in social enterprises and real estate.

While we are grateful for the recognition, however, we won't rest until there is an ASH location in every major metropolitan city in the country, and a shift in the paradigm on how our nation addresses the issues of poverty, homelessness, and behavioral health. We look into the eyes of people like Nicole and know we are making a difference. Working in finance, I learned to recognize a good investment when I saw it and I know our model of investing in a system that heals the complex issues of our most vulnerable people, in their time of greatest need, offers a priceless payoff for every American.

MENTORSHIP MOMENT

Here are a few of my secrets to success I've learned from founding ASH.

Research, Then Think Like a Visionary. Do your homework on your industry, competitive landscape, economic factors, and especially, the key players. Charisma and credentials do not substantiate someone's past. Then, think proactively. What is the data telling you? What can you infer will happen next? Where is the opportunity? How can you benefit?

If the Vision Doesn't Exist, Create It. When we couldn't find a path for people addicted to drugs to right themselves, we created one. When we couldn't find employers to hire our residents, we built social enterprises. When we couldn't find affordable apartments, we developed some. Do you see a gap in the market? Can you create a solution? Who should you partner with to accomplish your goal?

Go for the Most Good. Start by considering support of an established, principled, and successful charity or social enterprise with a good track record before starting your own. We could not find a model aligning with our values, so we had to create ASH. Don't try to reinvent the wheel. Instead, partner, donate, or volunteer to support what works or help scale what's already working.

Align your Vision & Values. When you face obstacles and challenges, stay true to who you are, and surround yourself with others who share your vision and values. Let your passion for your vision inspire others and get you through the tough times. Enjoy the journey!

BIOGRAPHY

Neli Vazquez Rowland is the co-founder and pioneering architect of A Safe Haven (ASH), an award-winning, vertically integrated, social and economic development model that rebuilds the lives of people impacted by poverty, behavioral healthcare, substance abuse, prison reentry, and homelessness with a holistic, individualized, case management approach. ASH provides multi-disciplinary services for opioid or heroin substance abuse treatment, education, healthcare, job training and placement, then offers phased, permanent, and affordable housing for residents to achieve sustainable independence.

Neli seeks to help inspire a "paradigm shift" on how America addresses social and economic issues by leveraging public and private investment resources for maximum return on investment (ROI) and social impact for stakeholders and those they serve.

Neli was named a "Champion of Change" by President

Obama in 2013, nominated by Rotary International, and introduced by President Trump as a featured speaker at the White House Opportunity Zone Conference in 2019.

Neli is a graduate of Loyola University, Chicago and the Tuck School of Business at Dartmouth, and enjoyed thirteen years in financial services prior to founding ASH. Neli serves on the board of the Illinois Chamber of Commerce and the Small Business Advocacy Council and is a highly sought-after public speaker. Neli is married to Brian Rowland, ASH Co-Founder and military veteran, and has two wonderful sons Devin and Dylan.

Neli Vazquez Rowland
www.NeliVazquezRowland.com
LinkedIn: /nelivazquezrowland
Twitter: @neli_Rowland

TOGETHER IS BETTER: FINDING THE RIGHT TEAM

Veronica Sosa

"You become the people you have around you."

My name is Verónica Sosa. I am the Founder of Business Fit International and Business Fit Magazine, Founder of SHE, (Seminar for Hispanic entrepreneurs) an organization which serves as a platform of visibility and connection for beginners and well-known entrepreneurs so they can be seen and heard. I own a cleaning company in Belgium and I collaborate with some amazing people, working in many more different projects. I am also an author, international speaker, award winner, and relational capital lover!

PLACES AND FACES

I was born in Venezuela on the 23rd of December in

1973. I had a comfortable childhood. My father was, and still is, a doctor and my mother, a lawyer. I have one brother and two sisters, and I am the eldest. When I was left in charge, I would tell my siblings that I was now "mother" and they had to do as I told them - this didn't always go down so well! But it was the first time I felt Iike a leader.

When I was 14, my parents got divorced and this was a difficult time for me. Once I had finished school, I started to study orthodontics to make my father happy, even though I knew it wasn't for me and gave it up after a year. It was always like this for me in Venezuela; I would start something, but never see it through.

I have never enjoyed monotonous things; always love to try and do different things. Spanish people have a term for this- - "the green dog of the house"—which is what they call people they consider weird. Recently, I have found another term for this, thanks to Emilie Wapnick – "multipotentialites" – people who work in many different areas at the same time.

The first major turning point in my life was when I was 18 years old. I persuaded my parents to let me sell the car they had bought me so I could go the United States and study English. When I returned to Venezuela, I fell in love and this person had an effect on who I am today. We were together for six years, but it was a destructive relationship. It was aggressive and physical, a sort of love/hate relationship, but I couldn't see this at the time. My family forced me to leave Venezuela and move to Gran Canaria to live with my brother to fully escape it. Then I became the leader of my life.

And life was good. It was exciting, different, and new. I was in the Canary Islands where there were a lot of young people, sun, beaches, parties, and lots of drinking. I had fun and I was happy; I lived the crazy life, danced, and earned a lot of money.

Initially, I worked in a bar. I lived a vampire's life, working at night and sleeping during the day. Then, I met the man who became my husband and I decided to look for a more stable job. I started working as a secretary in an English advertising company, but within six months they had recognized my potential and I was running the business. I was now a leader of other people.

I discovered I have a creative mind. I'm an innovator, a generator of ideas, and able to grasp a macro vision for business. I enjoyed building relationships and helping my clients with their projects.

I was then hired by a German company that asked me to be the Sales and Marketing Director for InfoCanaria because they liked the way I dealt with people. My salary increased considerably, and I felt I was experiencing dramatic growth. What I didn't realize at the time was that I was growing on the outside. I was not taking care of the damaged child within.

Two years later, my husband suggested we move to Belgium, where he was from. We believed this would be better for my daughter, so I agreed. I naïvely thought it would be easy for me to continue my life in a similar way to the one I was leaving. I couldn't have been more wrong.

SPANISH IN EUROPE

In a short amount of time, I went from being an accomplished, successful entrepreneur, who was stable and secure, to becoming the exact opposite. I became this horrible woman, where everything was a problem—the weather, the cold, the language barrier—everything was an issue. I had no car, my clothes weren't appropriate for the climate, and nobody would employ me since I didn't speak Dutch or French. I hit rock bottom and no longer recognized myself in the mirror. Who was I? Who had I become? Where had my relentless nature and fighting spirit gone? Where was the clown and joker?

Eventually, to try and help myself, I took to Facebook, something I had mainly avoided up to that point. I searched for groups of Hispanics or those addressing depression so I could talk to people who were in the same position as me. In one group for Venezuelans, I saw an advertisement looking for dancers. I have always loved dancing. I used to choreograph dances for my cousins and I have a vivid memory of when I was three, dancing with my father to Donna Summer's *I Feel Love*. I don't have many recollections of my parents being happy together, but I do remember this one occasion, both laughing as we danced. It is a precious memory of a beautiful moment and dancing has always made me happy.

So, although I was in my late 30's, I met with the woman who had placed the advertisement. A Venezuelan group needed two dancers for a gig they were doing in Holland. It was a one-off thing, and I agreed to do it. It was a start.

Unable to speak the local language, I couldn't get a job working for someone else, so I began giving Zumba classes. Then the woman I had danced with suggested I join a group called Digital Apprentice, where I could learn about marketing, digital marketing, social media etc. It didn't matter that I couldn't speak the local language; I could start an online business. Soon, I had plans to become an internet consultant in English or Spanish. However, my career took a different direction.

In 2014, me and two other friends saw an opportunity to create a Spanish-speaking event for professional Hispanic women. All the events in Central Europe were in English, so we were pioneers by giving voice to Spanish-speaking women. Our event provided a place to speak and present classes. Our first event was in Amsterdam, with 50 women attending. We were so proud and happy about this achievement.

I also created Business Fit International, running it in parallel with SHE, but in English, working with a coach. I had paid for a course as an international speaker, so he took me everywhere. I travelled to Norway, Sweden, Iceland, and Denmark. In the U.S., I spoke in Orlando and Los Angeles, and I went to South Africa and Spain.

The second SHE event was in 2016 with Ismael Cala. It was an amazing event, but it also became apparent that the three original owners didn't work well together. I ended up taking on SHE alone, with my first solo event in 2018 at the Radisson Blue Hotel in Amsterdam with 150 women attending. It will take place once again on October 12, 2019 in Belgium. In addition,

I am creating clubs in other European cities, comprised of 20 to 30 women, to perpetuate the momentum of the main event. The clubs give women an opportunity to share ideas and create joint ventures, discuss innovation, and what is new in the market. So far, we have clubs in Germany, the UK, Spain, and Belgium. I will also be travelling to South America to create a movement for woman to feel empowered and discuss gender equality and women's rights, as it is still a very macho environment there.

SHAPING UP WITH BUSINESS FIT

Business Fit Magazine was created in 2016. I was very interested in being fit, particularly crossfit, so I had the idea that you should keep your Business Fit as well as your body. The first edition was terrible and maybe one day I will be able to laugh at it. But since then, I have been growing and trying to find the right people to create pillars to show entrepreneurs how to develop themselves, their business, their ideas and their vision to create a business with purpose.

When I began this new journey into entrepreneurship, I also started to look into personal development, and this has put me on a path of learning to respect others and understand them. However, I do believe the first step towards self-development is to respect ourselves.

I wanted to surround myself with people who brought out the best in me. I believe you become the people you have around you. So I wanted to encircle myself with people who love me, want me to succeed, who aren't interested in gossiping and negativity, and who are creators and want to help others.

Sometimes, as an entrepreneur, you may have to sacrifice something. All this personal growth and development created change in me. I finally started to take care of all of my internal issues and my limiting beliefs. This time I grew on the inside. But my husband did not. He stayed the same, and he didn't believe in internal growth. All the time I thought I had his support, I was wrong. He had felt alone, but never said anything. So just as I was starting to feel alive and find myself, I received the devastating news that he had been cheating on me. It was another kick in the teeth, but it gave me the strength to say: Really? Look at me, boy!

I spent the next three years, separated, doing my thing and him doing his. We took care of our daughter as parents, but we were apart. In couples, sometimes one grows more than the other. My husband never believed in personal development or what I believed in, and that split us apart. Now I believe we have taken different paths, even though he was my mirror when I was younger. He isn't anymore; we want different things.

I travelled a lot and wrote a book with some ladies around the world called From Fed up to Fabulous. I got to meet famous people: Vanilla Ice, 50 Cent, Calvin Klein, Mark Zuckerberg's sister, Randi. I started investing in some coaches. Not all of them worked out but I still learned from them. They showed me what I didn't want to do.

In the past, I have not always made smart connections. My motto is "together is better," and I cannot emphasize enough the importance of building a really good team. Not everyone has the same values you do. It is challenging to build the right team, but it is vital to succeed.

I have encountered women who don't walk the talk, which to me is so important. In my opinion, you cannot create a female community or sorority when you are a leader who wants to shine above everything and everyone else. That's what I call building a pyramid to showcase yourself. I step away from these leaders. I don't want to be part of those groups, and I don't believe in leading that way. To me, that is a patriarchal movement.

One woman I wanted to collaborate with had created a woman's movement. Unfortunately, we had a conflict of interest, so she just forbade my entrance to her conferences. That really hurt me. Even if someone wants to work in the same industry as me, I would help them and create a situation where we would all win. It makes me sad when people work against others rather than with them. I understand not all people like my energy, but I would never put someone down if I didn't like their energy. But I do believe there are more good people with dreams and love and values than bad ones.

I have been lucky enough to have many angels in my life, those people who have helped guide me. My grandmother was the first person I admired. She was a divorced teacher who became involved in politics, which women in Venezuela weren't allowed to do in those days. My mother showed me the true love of a parent. I realize now how painful it must have been for her to extricate me from a destructive relationship and send me away. Vikki Thomas is my soul sister and we have worked together on many projects. Viola Edward, my psychotherapist, introduced me to Breathwork, and Jacqueline Camacho-Ruiz believed in me enough to bring her movement to Europe. Ismael Cala is the biggest angel I have been blessed with. He gave me an opportunity by trusting and believing in me. Ervin László introduced me to the Akasha Paradigms. And I have also learned from my mentees; I teach them, then they teach me back. It's all a cycle.

TAKING CARE

For me, one of the most important things is to take care of yourself and the people around you, which includes family, friends, colleagues, and your business. It's a balance which can be quite difficult. You need to take control of your time and make it happen. It's like dancing. You need to learn how to delegate so you can concentrate on what you are good at. It can be difficult finding the right people who also believe in your dream, believe in you, and connect with you. In the beginning those were my challenges, but now I have learned how to be the leader and to let people lead in their areas of expertise.

Success is finding the right people to work with who can do the things you aren't able to do. But as an entrepreneur, even if you are delegating, you must have a little bit of knowledge about what the other people are doing. Ultimately, though, dedicate yourself to what you do best. What I do best is connect and create platforms in English and Spanish.

To create a great team, you need to have a manifesto with

steps for everyone to follow. For me, the core values for my team to adopt are honesty, loyalty, love, and the ability to work together, and support each other. I need to work with people who realize they don't know everything (just like me) but who are open to learn, grow, love, and succeed.

For me, Sir Isaac Newton's quote sums up how to grow. He said, "If I have seen further than others, it is by standing on the shoulders of giants." Learning from the people above me is how I have been inspired to move forward. The people you surround yourself with truly matter.

When you reach rock bottom, you can die or you can take another breath, move on, and find someone to take your hand to help you out. If you have done the right thing and you have values, love, and have given, you will have plenty of people around to help you when you need it.

When I have had the most difficult times, I have felt protected by my family, friends, and people who work with me and support me. When you love and receive love back, it is the most powerful tool; it is magic. Love makes you move and grow and shine and smile. That is what I believe. When I have been in the most terrifying place, I have felt people supporting me and that makes me move forward.

The key to success is to believe in yourself, and this can be difficult at times. There are three things which work against you. First of all, yourself, including your fears and doubt. You need to find yourself and know what you want. If necessary, find a good coach to help you in your search. When what you think, say, and do are all aligned and you have congruency in your life, things start to change.

The second thing which can work against you is the people around you. Family may be afraid you won't succeed so they may try to stop you so that you don't have to experience failure. But failure is an amazing thing. It shows you when something isn't right and that you should try it another way. Through disappointment, you keep trying. How many times did Edison fail before he finally created the electric light bulb?

The third thing which can work against you is people outside your immediate circle – who don't understand why you want to change. When I started organizing conferences, people who I knew when I was younger would message me with an air of disbelief. People find change to be bad and hard to accept. People want you to remain in your comfort zone.

Always follow your intuition. It is the most powerful tool we have, and we often don't listen to it. Instead, we take the more logical path, which can lead us to a lesser place. Never underestimate your intuition.

My businesses have helped me to grow, believe in myself, and feed my soul and body. Everything that I learn in *Business Fit* and SHE helps me to stay on track. I do believe in the Mayan calendar and I read a lot. I have rituals, now more than ever, to keep moving forward.

My dream is to co-create things with many people. I love to connect with people from the soul. I do believe in love, in acknowledging emotions, breathwork, body, mind and soul fitness. This is what I want to teach so I can help people improve. It has also helped me. My businesses have helped me to grow and believe in myself, to feed my soul and body.

MENTORSHIP MOMENT

Take time now to slow down and reflect on some of the concepts I have shared in this story.

1. How do you defuse fear when it threatens to keep you from success?
2. Who are the "giants" that you stand on to go further in your life and career?
3. Have you ever had a language barrier or been the outsider, the foreigner, the intruder? How did it hinder your success? What did you do about it?
4. Are you a "multipotentialite?" Is it a blessing or a curse to be one?
5. Do you believe failure can be an "amazing" thing? Why or why not?

BIOGRAPHY

Verónica Sosa is the Founder of Business Fit International and Business Fit Magazine, and SHE (Seminar for Hispanics Entrepreneurs in Europe), an author, international speaker, award winner, and relational capital lover. She has more than 18 years experience in the editorial and corporate sectors as a Marketing and Sales Manager for international publicity companies in Spain.

Verónica is dedicated to empowering women and helping them rediscover themselves and live a better life. With marketing, branding online, and international business expertise, she teaches others to create "clarity" in their personal and professional lives to succeed and create business with purpose. She has given conferences in Relational Capital in South Africa, Norway, Sweden, Finland, Iceland, Spain, Holland, France, Cyprus, and North America. Her organization, SHE, helps Hispanic women achieve their goals and balance their body, mind, and spirit to achieve results and congruence in life.

Verónica is one of six authors of the book *From Fed up to Fabulous*, which helps women find their purpose in life. She is an international motivational speaker and inspires audiences to reach their highest potential. The Verónica Sosa Foundation, Fundastrea, provides support and education to women in need, and is based in Venezuela.

Veronica Sosa

info@hispanasemprendedoras.eu

www.meetveronicasosa.com

Instagram: @veronicasosac

GROWING LEADERSHIP IN ANY ENVIRONMENT

___

Michelle Rohrer-Lauer

"Leading means sharing your vision and values with others."

I was only 17 years old when the wall-mounted house phone rang and my mom took the call. It was someone at nearby Illinois Masonic Hospital telling us that my father was in intensive care. My heart sank to my stomach. My parents had divorced when I was only two but he had always been in my life. My father was a sweet, loving man, but unfortunately, his alcoholism and compulsive gambling had taken a toll on the marriage. Now my mother worked two jobs to support us and we lived in a tough, suburban neighborhood—so tough that I was bussed the five blocks to school because of the danger. It was a toxic environment but I learned how to survive it by holding my head up high when I had to walk through the scariest of places.

As we raced to the hospital, I still felt his hug from the last time I saw him and his deep voice telling me he loved me. Would I hear it again? When we arrived, we saw him lying lifeless, in a coma on the bed, tubes radiating from various parts of his body, including the cruel tracheotomy protruding skyward from his throat. I learned that he had been brutally beaten, but we did not know who did it.

As I reached out and gently touched his hand, all I could do was pray. Then I heard the low, ominous tones of the doctor conversing with my mom, saying that he didn't think my dad would make it and if he did, he would be a vegetable. In the morning, my father was gone, dead from the injuries he sustained and murdered by someone who was never caught.

I never knew our last hug was really the last. And I never got to say goodbye. But it was a life-changing moment for me because I realized I needed to make a change and get out of the neighborhood. My father had a disease, but I had choices. I needed to take advantage of every opportunity and everything I had learned thus far to follow my heart and my ambitions wherever they would lead. I knew what I wanted to do. I just didn't know how to do it. But I would get there to make him proud.

DESIGNING A LIFE

Some people know what they are born to do. In my case, I was a born interior designer but didn't know it. Who else would turn a Barbie doll case on its side to create a living room, using handkerchiefs for area rugs?

Being an only child, I played by myself often and took delight in creating beautiful spaces for Barbie. I would look around my room, see what I had to work with and design the perfect living room for her. My smallest drawers from my Barbie case served as sofas. I would dive under the kitchen table, draped with a blanket, to create a luxurious living space with a roof and a second floor, courtesy of the chairs. There was a hole in the middle of the table and a pillow inside it which made a fluffy, comfy bed that would be the envy of Skipper and Ken.

I loved to change my environment. When my mother came home from work, she would often find the living room rearranged and she would like it better! I always volunteered to wrap the Christmas gifts with a festive style all my own. It seemed I was always leading others to beauty. My Mom called me a leader, and would tell me that when she saw me with my friends, I was the one leading the pack with the big idea. As for my mom, she was a leader in our household and my role model of positive energy which I bring to my own leadership style today. She taught me to always see the glass as half full.

When I was 14, my mother gave me a room of my own. I was in designer heaven! Instinctively, I latched on to the starting point of design with a focal point—my lively, lime green comforter with red and black ladybugs on it—and I chose my room's color palette off that comforter. I draped a whimsical wall of green beads across my doorway which matched the green fringe on my bedroom light fixture and shone on my walls covered with Tiger Beat magazine posters of Donny Osmond.

While mom was a bookkeeper and the analytical sort, her sister, Aunt Helen, was an oil painter with an artistic eye. She was blown away by the creative expression of my decorating and asked me if there was ever anything about it I wanted to change. I replied, "Always." And then she told me that she felt the same way as a painter, and she taught me that we are never done with our creations. We are always learning when it comes to creating a beautiful environment.

Leadership is the same. Leaders are always learning and tweaking, based on our experiences. I believe a leader who stops learning is following, which is one reason I'm always seeking continuing education through conferences, presentations, etc. When I first started out in the industry, I didn't know what I didn't know. After five years I knew a lot, but not as much as I did after a decade. Now, thanks to my experience, my resourcefulness and having the right team, I lead by staying aware of changing trends and people's buying habits to offer people what they want most. I also lead by example, pitching in and doing whatever it takes for the customer and the company.

I've loved every minute of the past 30 years working in interior design, but I never anticipated being an entrepreneur. I just knew I could sell and I wanted to design exciting spaces.

After design school, those two factors landed me in a high-end furniture store where I met other like-minded people and helped customers design their spaces. But I also paid attention to the customers who were looking for high-end baby and juvenile furniture and could not find a good selection anywhere. That's when I decided to go into business with Betty, another designer and friend at the store. Our plan was to open up our own baby and juvenile furniture boutique together.

ADVENTURES IN BUSINESS

Our boutique, the Stork Room, was a magical place in Libertyville, Illinois. I reveled in leading new parents to a beautify furnished room for their children. At first, it was up to Betty and I to do it all. We sold, inventoried, ordered, received shipments and then delivered furniture to our patron's homes. Everything was our job and we were a tight team that would do whatever it took to make the customer happy.

As we grew and hired people to help with all aspects of the business, including the physical work, we led by example and showed how the Stork Room must differentiate itself by offering stellar customer service. That meant every employee needed to pitch in and do what was right for the customer, even if it wasn't in the employee's "job description." There were times when someone wouldn't come in and I was delivering furniture in a suit because I had just come from a client meeting. There were customers who would scream at us because their baby bumper was going to come in a day late, but we all smiled and bore it pleasantly and learned that you can't please every person all of the time. All you can do is your best.

We opened in 1985. Six months later, the Bears won the Superbowl and we found out we were in the middle of Chicago Bears country. Some of them patronized the store and they were all delightful, down-to-earth gentlemen. I'll never forget the day William Perry (a.k.a. The Fridge) asked to pick up his order rather than have us deliver it to his house. He drove up with his SUV and we led him to the heavy, solid wood, ornate dresser and offered to load it for him. After all, we had loaded many of his team members' cars in the past. He just said "no thanks," and lifted it over his head and placed it on top the SUV like it was an oversized stuffed animal he had won at the carnival! Talk about someone going above and beyond!

We also learned the importance of hiring a team that works well together. At our high point we had nine employees. When the mix of personalities was just right, the store reverberated with good vibrations and positive energy. Laughter filled the air and we knew our people were enjoying themselves. But when someone left and was replaced, often the dynamic would completely change, energy would fall, and sometimes, productivity would suffer.

I still think hiring people is one of the most difficult things I have had to do as a business owner. We wanted an employee that would go the extra mile for the pregnant shopper or stay late to receive a shipment for an important customer. I wanted to know if they would say "can I help you?" or "that's not my job."

After several years, the market for juvenile furniture began to change. Large discounters like Toys R' Us and mail order retailers were now selling cribs. Betty, who was 20 years older than me, was looking to retire. As for me, I was ready for more too. It was time to close the Stork Room.

Saying goodbye was bittersweet. One of the most lovely things about the business was getting to know the customers and sharing in their joy of preparing for a new child. We knew their stories. We grew with them as their babies first crossed our threshold in their mother's stomach to buy a crib, then in a stroller to buy more accessories, and one day toddling in on their own two feet to pick out the "big boy bed." We crossed our fingers and prayed with our clients for their adoption to come through. And we rushed our Jewish client's baby furniture to their nursery once their baby was born, as was tradition.

Today the brick and mortar experience continues to fade from our retail landscape, and I for one will miss the customer service, the experience of being guided through a sales process and of course, the ability to touch and feel what you order before you buy it. But life is change, and change was in the air.

I started Michelle's Interiors in my basement with two employees because one thing I had learned from being in business was that I needed help to do it right. Leaders understand their gifts and help others rise to their potential. That's why I also knew it was most important to spend the bulk of my time in business development.

I was also starting the business in the dawn of the digital

age. My fax machine began to grow idle as more and more of my vendors sent their estimates by email instead. My Blackberry became my new lifeline. I learned to read the newfangled emails off the monitor instead of printing them. Soon our operation moved out of my home to a small office, only to be replaced years later by my renovated home with a small, shared office space, where I am based today.

In sharp contrast to the cold, impersonal feel of the new email, I brought warm, classic look to my branding, with beautiful, eye appealing stationary and envelopes that bore a sophisticated design and were silky to the touch. I wanted my correspondence to stand out in the pile, and it did with clean, modern red and black lines and a solid red, back flap on the envelope. Everything about it bespoke quality and I still hold my brand to those high standards today.

NO PLACE LIKE HOME

I learned best how to pull together a team and plan a large project when my husband and I built a house together with our own two hands! It was 1983, and as environment is important to me, our goal was to build a home affordably, using top quality materials and saving money on labor.

With the moxy I developed from my childhood environment, I walked into the bank myself and asked the president of the bank for a loan. With a smirk, he declared that we would never finish the project, but if we could do it in six months, we could have the loan. Beyond that, he could get us a mortgage. I told him we would keep our deadline and I meant it.

Our former 2,100 square foot home in Lake Villa is not only finished, but still standing, and constructed with exceptional quality, just as we planned. We used 2" x 6" framing instead of 2" x 4"s and thicker, better quality concrete mix for the foundation. We insulated the interior walls and installed high quality casement windows. We subcontracted the electrical, plumbing and some other items, but most of the interior and exterior of the house was built to our exact specifications for us, by us, while still both working full time jobs. There were times our neighbors witnessed us drive up after work and shine the headlights of our cars on the house as we finished up an exterior project.

The knowledge I gained about home construction eventually made me a better designer. I learned the importance of scheduling and bringing a small team of contractors together. I learned to stay focused, work with architects and other professionals that bring a home to life, and meet a tight deadline. Best of all, we kept our word to the bank and exceeded not only their expectations, but ours too. Leaders are consistent and keep their promises, which is exactly what we did.

Leading also means sharing your vision and values with others. For example, everyone who works with me knows I believe surroundings are everything. I have always held fast to this tenet even when I only had Barbie to work with or when I was a young single without a lot of money. Somehow, everyone wanted to hang at my house because of the inviting way I would decorate my apartment space.

Your surroundings should be beautiful because design is important to our well being and our ability to thrive. Beautifully designed surroundings invite us, comfort us, and make us happy. Think of the way hospitals have been redesigned over the years, with luxurious birthing suites for new mothers and comfy chairs for visitors. We often take the beauty of our surroundings for granted, but picture your favorite restaurant. Picture the environment of the restaurant, everything you love, and then your favorite dinner on the menu. Now be honest. Would you enjoy it as much if you had to eat it in a McDonald's? It may not even taste the same to you!

Over time, I learned I could design a room that could improve a client's everyday life and help them thrive and create a more healthy lifestyle. It all made sense. A crowded, cluttered kitchen will silently beg for the owners to call for take-out. A beautifully designed kitchen with everything accessible and easy to use will invite a cook to step in and cook a beautiful meal in record time. Choosing natural fabrics can actually improve air quality in a household, and everyone knows that a home gym increases the likelihood of daily exercise.

I learned and taught that while we may spend weeks planning our vacation, we often do not even spend a few hours planning our most important surroundings—our home, where we raise our children. Home should be our vacation area, our retreat. We should walk through the door at the end of the day and feel as happy and comfortable as we would entering a luxurious vacation home. I share this vision with each client and lead them to a better, more liveable, and even healthier environment.

HEART'S DESIRE FULFILLED

I think my dad would be proud of where I am today. I have shared my experience of his loss as a volunteer with RAINBOWS, a support organization for children who have experienced loss or are weathering life's storms. It makes me feel good to help children through their personal struggles but also see how my experience can be placed in a positive light, to pass on the appreciation for life that my father once had and I do as well.

About six months after he passed, I was working at my summer job for the Waukegan Park District. There was a young woman who mowed the park property and she would bring her darling, three-year-old daughter with her. One day I just couldn't resist saying, "Your daughter is so adorable." And then, she went on to tell me that the little girl, like me, had just lost her father, but in a car crash just weeks earlier.

At that moment, I took it as a sign and knew I was blessed. I knew my father loved me, and was waiting for me to follow my heart and make something of myself. If he were alive today, I think he'd like what he'd see, the leader I've become and the way I help others create environments in which they can thrive.

MENTORSHIP MOMENT

Leaders who create productive, positive environments will thrive and so will their employees. Here are some questions to help you reflect on your environment and if it is helping your team (and you!) be all they can be.

1. How would you describe the energy in the environment you lead? In what way can you make it even more positive?

2. I was raised in a tough neighborhood where I learned to cover up fear and make the most of and be thankful for what I was given. How has your upbringing helped you become the leader you are today?

3. What are some ways you lead by example, modeling behavior for your team that you want exhibited in your organization? How can you do this in a regular way?

BIOGRAPHY

Michelle is an award-winning interior and furniture design professional with more than 30 years experience providing innovative design solutions to prominent clients nationwide. Michelle believes that every homeowner has the right to a well-designed home that feels like a vacation retreat and will reduce stress, increase healthy living, and improve overall well-being.

She has designed unique, one-of-a-kind residential interiors for Fortune 500 company executives, CEOs and successful entrepreneurs in Chicagoland and nationwide, and has won considerable acclaim for her special projects and furniture pieces. Michelle designed the game rooms that were awarded as grand prizes in a Kraft Foods national sweepstakes. Her award-winning creations include a submarine bed, a skateboard-themed bunk bed, a "Rat Pack" card table, retro media centers, and a variety of custom banquettes.

Michelle mastered her craft working with more than

700 residential clients and designing several small commercial projects. These experiences have sharpened her understanding of a wide range of cultures and lifestyles and ability to handle the most difficult design challenges.

Michelle's work has been featured in trade publications nationwide, Chicago newspapers, Martha Stewart Radio, and TV outlets ranging from WGN and local NBC and ABC affiliates to HGTV.

Michelle Rohrer-Lauer

michelle@michelleinteriors.com

Instagram: @michellesinteriors

Facebook: Michelle's Interiors Design Group

LEADING WITH GRATITUDE: A #PILOTINA'S TAKE-OFFS AND LANDINGS

—

Jackie Camacho-Ruiz

"There is no more significant life than a life that serves others."

It was December of 2006, I was only twenty-three years old, and it was the second time I had heard the horrible word, "cancer" from my doctor. The first time was when I was diagnosed at twenty-one years old. The solution required two surgeries within two weeks. To be that close to the unimaginable loss of being able to bear children as a newlywed still shakes me when I think about it.

Now my doctor was telling me I had Extrahepatic Choledocal Cyst Type II, the second rarest out of five different types of cysts (very common in Japan). One in one hundred fifty thousand people get it in this part of the hemisphere. I had no relative of Japanese descent. It made no sense at all, yet there it was. Surgery was a must, as indicated from a mysterious series of pain attacks that began after I chose to "cleanse my palate" with a cardamom seed at an Indian restaurant. We thought it was an allergic reaction at first but after two weeks of exploration at Northwestern Hospital, we found out it was much more.

"We will have to operate," he said decisively, and he explained the complications that could arise—bile leaking into the intestinal system, organs disintegrating--and how serious the outcome could be. In short, the surgery was life-threatening.

I had heard him. But at that moment, I could not accept defeat or even conceive of it. "But I need to be out in time for my finals," I replied, only thinking of how I was a breath away from completing my marketing degree at the College of DuPage that year. "I'm graduating with honors and I have to finish." My face told him I was serious and meant business. And in reply, his face softened as he grappled with the difference between my attitude and the gravity of the situation.

"Jackie, it's important you go home and spend this Christmas with your family," he said. "We'll do the surgery in January."

Something in his tone gave me goosebumps and I grasped what he was saying. Yet we both knew I wasn't about to lose hope. I was a fighter. And I had three weeks with my family.

THE MISSION

I've always been someone with a positive attitude, driven to climb the next mountain or create one for myself! But it wasn't until this second bout with cancer that I really understood why I had been put on this earth, and how that positive attitude would help fuel my true purpose.

After my first diagnosis when I was twenty-one, I vowed to never take another day for granted and I never have since. I now experience life with a sprinkle of wonder and gratitude, savoring the magic in a touch from my children and a caress from my husband, a loving talk with a good friend or the beauty of the landscape whether I see it from eye level or thirty thousand feet, and helping someone succeed in their business...it's all beautiful and part of my appreciation for life.

I cherished everything in those vital three weeks before my surgery. I spent the Christmas of 2006 with the knowledge that it might be my last. Nevertheless, I celebrated with family, telling them how much I loved them and hearing the same said to me. I had my share of tears, and laughter through tears too. Surely this surgery would not take me from my new husband, who was the love of my life, and my small son who needed his mother.

During this second surgery, I dreamed a vivid dream. I was having an out-of-body experience, flying over Lake

Michigan, soaring through the clouds with a feeling of peace, yet exhilaration from the joy of feeling free. And then….

"I think she's awake." It was a nurse standing over me, like an angel, with a pleasant smile. I was in a hospital room with a freeway of tubes snaking in and out of my body; a catheter, feeding tube and intravenous drip. Soon my surgeon was there too. "Jackie, your positive attitude saved you," he said, looking down at me as I focused on him, as the awareness that my operation was over washed over me. "Your cyst was pre-cancer level four. You were born with it and could have died without knowing about it except when you ate that cardamom seed, it caused the cyst to swell so that it obstructed the passage of bile. That brought on the pain and other complications."

He went on, and I could hear the incredulousness in his voice as he explained how I had come so close to losing everything. Again, I had been saved. I was going to be fine, he told me and I repeated it back to myself. I AM ALIVE.

Then they left me alone. I was grateful for the luxury of privacy to reflect on the doctor's words. I looked up at the white ceiling and in that room I was suddenly given a message in my heart. It was a message that would guide me the rest of my life.

"You are here to serve others."

God's message was clear. And the message became my mission.

JOURNEY TO SERVANT LEADER

Ever since that day, I have worked to serve others, creating community, mentoring, giving, and elevating others through my talents and resources. I have done my best to always approach people as a servant leader.

A servant leader is a person who thinks about others first and being a leader second. They prioritize the growth and prosperity of those around them, and help with other's needs, rather than feeding their own personal ambitions. Being a servant leader is about community building and lifting up your fellow workers. Caring for other people is the greatest strength of a servant leader. Servant leaders make a conscious choice to promote the growth and well-being of the people they lead. It's not about being "at the top of the pyramid;" it's about helping the others climb up to the top by developing their skills and passions.

It's easy to become a servant leader if you just look around. Ask yourself, what can I do to help those around me, and make them more productive?

I've always been a "make it happen" type of person, a dreamer who is continually setting productive goals for myself. In 2010, I achieved one of my dreams, which was to become a published author with *The Little Book of Business Secrets that Work.* In it I shared the lessons I had learned as a young entrepreneur. I followed with a memoir, *The Fig Factor.*

In that story, I relate how as a little girl growing up in Mexico City, I was always fascinated by entrepreneurship. We had a fig tree in our backyard and I used to sell my figs to the people passing by on the street. I read at an early age and even back then, enjoyed the wisdom of Napoleon Hill and Dale Carnegie.

My mother was an entrepreneurial role model for me, selling cosmetics in the community. She used to take me on her sales calls and sometimes, would let me do part of her presentation. I can trace my love of public speaking and motivating audiences to those experiences.

I had come to America when I was fourteen years old and was determined to learn the language (which I did within months) and succeed. I aspired to go to college and have a career in marketing and succeeded, founding my marketing firm with my husband Juan Pablo, JJR Marketing, in 2006. But as I achieved these goals, I started to notice the young Latinas in Chicago and the surrounding suburbs and how they often felt unable to reach their dreams, simply because they did not know how, or they had perceived barriers that could actually be easily overcome with the right educational path or mentorship. The idea of all these young ladies feeling trapped, with no access to their goals, was unacceptable to me. I had to do something.

April eleventh is my birthday and I was coming up on the big "three-one." At the time, I was doing marketing for Medieval Times, the dinner theater experience. I decided to throw a "princess birthday party" at Medieval Times for thirty-one young ladies, complete with tiaras. In a group, we gathered and talked about our visions for the future and the goals we can set to make them happen. It was the seed that germinated into the Fig Factor Foundation.

The Fig Factor Foundation is the nonprofit I started in 2014 that is dedicating to unleashing the "amazing" in young

Latinas, age twelve to twenty-five. The two-day program contains four key components: ACTIVATE (allowing Latinas to identify and study the eight fig factors of personal development as discussed in my book), RECEIVE (where mentors work with them for six months to make progress towards their goals), GROW (where graduates are provided with connections between the graduate, the community, and its opportunities) and SHARE (where they give back to the community through service). To date, we have had nearly one hundred and thirty young ladies go through the program, then go on to achieve their dreams.

April eleventh is still my birthday but now it is also "Young Latina" Day around Chicagoland. In 2017, we got a declaration from the mayor of Aurora to declare April eleventh "Young Latina Day", and in 2019, six more cities followed suit! On Young Latina Day, young Latinas, their participants and their mentors receive the declaration from legislators at municipal centers throughout the suburbs. It has been a wonderful triumph for the organization and a way for young Latinas to feel validated in their home communities.

I also recognized that many of the Latinas I met in the business world may or may not have had mentors and role models themselves. Many of them also had unfortunate immigrant experiences but went on to achieve the "American Dream" despite their adversities. They had incredible stories to tell, and I wanted to help them do it. So I created the *Today's Inspired Latina* book series.

The anthology series features approximately twenty-five

separate stories of Latinas in each volume who were unwilling to let obstacles stop the pursuit of their dreams. They are poignant stories of triumph and tears, and six years later, we are working on our sixth volume of the book! We're proud that more than one hundred and forty authors have had a platform to tell their story and reach their dream of becoming a published author. For many of the ladies in the books, their chapters have become springboards to new careers, speaking engagements, full-length solo book projects, podcasts, the founding of nonprofits, and more!

Most amazingly, *Today's Inspired Latina* has spawned a movement. What started with me asking ten Chicago area women if they would participate in the first book has grown to scores of women asking me if they can be in the next book. Women are no longer just from the Chicago area but from all over the U.S. and now, across the globe! Our next volume will feature authors from Europe, with Latina authors from countries such as Spain, Belgium, Italy, and Sweden.

It seems the more I try to do for people, the more they seem to receive from the universe. Some people would say it is luck or coincidence, but I say it is being open to the goodness of the people around you, never giving up on your dreams, and always doing what you can to help others. Also, sometimes when you surround yourselves with servant leaders, you will be folded into their radiance and start receiving yourself.

I have been invited back to my hometown in Mexico on several occasions to speak to groups of young Latinas. I began to dream of building a community center there, dedicated to the empowerment of the young ladies in the town. As I dined with a few dignitaries from the community, I voiced my idea and a lady in my midst who was a developer, said, "I'll give you the land." Incredible! Now my center is becoming a reality and we are close to breaking ground. It's just one example of the amazing things that have come my way as I have pursued my path of servant leadership.

On a day to day basis, I serve others by always listening with an ear towards assisting them in getting what they need, whether it is a vendor in search of the ideal client, a nonprofit in search of a sponsor, or an employee with a dream. I always try to connect people who can help each other whenever I can. We are set on this earth to help each other. We can all be servant leaders. And there is no more significant life than a life that serves others.

FLYING HIGH

The first time I was in a small sports plane was in 2015 with David Spano of SimplyFly, a flight school based out of Sugar Grove. The aircraft was like a lightweight, beautiful bird, and I was nervous but excited to take a ride. It felt nothing like flying in a large airplane. I was instantly and viscerally connected to it all--the exhilarating take-off and watching the ground disappear behind us, and then the quieting soar across the landscape I had driven on so many times but never fully appreciated. I felt connected, at peace, as gratitude for the experience and the beauty and wonder of it all touched my soul. And then, another dream took hold.

I decided to pursue my pilot's license. This would be a daunting task for anyone, let alone a mother with husband and two kids, CEO of a marketing company and a publishing house and executive director of a nonprofit. Yet the call to earn my license harkened back to that day in the hospital when I had the vision of flying over Lake Michigan. No wonder I wanted to fly. Flying was a symbol of something comforting, a sign that everything was going to be all right.

The journey to becoming a pilot includes a lot of "ground training" involving classroom work and study before you can even think about flying. A dear friend wishing to offer support to me on my journey presented me with a very special co-pilot—a teddy bear named Amelia, to be with me in support in place of my friend. As I studied for my written test, Amelia was there. When I planned my first cross country run, Amelia was there. When I did my first solo, Amelia was there with me, buckled in for emotional support. With her soft brown eyes and ready-to-hug body in celebration or disappointment, she helped me keep my eye on the prize. She stood for something bigger than myself.

Back on the ground, my wonderful husband, Juan Pablo, my children Leo and Giullianna, and my dear, late friend Lynn Torre cheered me on as I completed my first solo flight. I fell into their arms feeling accomplished, loved and joyful.

Being a licensed sports pilot is nothing short of amazing. It was even more amazing when I found out that of the licensed sport plane pilots in the country, less than two percent are Latina.

That's why I proudly tout the hashtag #pilotina!

I have learned so much from flying, but one of the most important things I have learned is perspective. Soaring a few thousand feet above the ground, I am "zoomed out" and it gives me a different perspective on my world. I try to bring this kind of dramatic shift in perspective back to Earth in order to fuse magic and practicality and make amazing things happen every day.

When I zoom out, I can conceive the magical possibilities beyond my idea. My zoomed out perspective showed me how *Today's Inspired Latina* could support a movement of Latina empowerment that would one day skip across the ocean to flourish on the European continent. It was my zoomed out perspective that let me envision and establish Fig Factor Media, a publishing house to help authors bring inspirational and significant stories to the world. It helped me see that I could also launch another book series, *Today's Inspired Leader*, which now debuts as my fourteenth book. The zoom out helps a leader visualize the magic. Without zooming out, the magic will never manifest.

You can't "zoom out" without "zooming in." Before I can zoom out to my stupendous view, I must adjust my perspective during my pre-flight preparation. Pre-flight requires inspections and checklists, focusing on the details so I can thrive. Once I get in mid-air, I am the master of my fate and my survival depends on how well I "zoomed in" as well as my skill as a pilot. At work, the zoom in means making sure sure my team is prepared with the right tools to do the job and our processes are airtight so we make deadlines and delight clients.

MORE TO GIVE

I have no idea what is in the future for me but I know that whatever beauty comes my way will be a result of my servant leadership. I am open to giving more, receiving more, and most of all, impacting as many people as I can before I leave this earth. I live in eternal and active gratitude to the hundreds of people who have touched my life in thoughtfulness, kindness, and through mentorship and example. Everything I have achieved I have done with the encouragement, love, and support of too many people to mention.

I still have much to do, big dreams to achieve and more to give the people who come my way, but I have a game plan on how to succeed. One of my early influencers, Napoleon Hill, wrote "It is true that you can succeed best and quickest by helping others to succeed." I have found nothing to be more true!

MENTORSHIP MOMENT

I'd like to share a formula that we use in the aviation world to help us prepare well for every flight: **PAVE**. Adopting PAVE in your business can keep you productive and flying high!

P is for PILOT. For a mission to succeed, you must have the right person in the cockpit! The people in charge must be well-trained, experienced, and impeccable at what they do. They need to know how to launch and land any project.

A is for AIRCRAFT. Do you have all the equipment you need for the project? Is it in working order? Nobody can fly well in an aircraft with missing or inoperable parts. We use checklists and other rituals to make sure everything is in order. What special procedures do you have in place to succeed each day?

V is for ENVIRONMENT. Pilots must learn a lot about the weather because it critically affects the safety, speed, and other aspects of a flight. In business, we must pay heed to the market environment and our competition. Are there storms on the horizon that could adversely affect sales? Is the competition causing us to reroute our trajectory? Are the skies clear, signaling a good time for accelerated growth? Navigate wisely and change course when necessary.

E is for EXTERNAL CIRCUMSTANCES. Unforeseen circumstances can ground our flight. On the job, here's when our "can do" attitude must kick in to forge ahead, change direction, reschedule the mission or "take the trip" anyway, even though circumstances aren't ideal.

BIOGRAPHY

Jacqueline Camacho-Ruiz embraces life and lives to elevate others. Having survived cancer twice, she went on to become an award-winning entrepreneur, international speaker, philanthropist and author of fourteen books. She is the CEO of JJR Marketing and The Fig Factor publishing house.

In 2014, her passion for inspiring young women led to the creation of The Fig Factor Foundation, a non-profit focused on unleashing the amazing in young Latinas. Her *Today's Inspired Latina* book series has given voice to more than one hundred authors and launched an international movement. Jackie has appeared on local and national TV shows like CBS World News, ESPN and Univision, radio shows and podcasts as well as in numerous magazines and newspapers including *Forbes* and *Inc* Magazine.

She is an international inspirational and keynote speaker and has addressed many Fortune 500 companies as well as the United States Army, BP International and United Airlines.

Jackie is married with two children and is a self-proclaimed "Pilotina," one of the few Latina small airplane pilots in the US.

Jacqueline Camacho-Ruiz

www.jackiecamacho.com

www.thefigfactor.org

#pilotina